MW01697617

As easy as Drinking Water

As easy as Drinking Water

A MUSLIM FORGIVEN

foreword by Rev. Dr. Patrick Safarian

AFSHIN JAVID

WinePressPublishing
Your Book, Defined.

WinePress Publishing (PO Box 428, Enumclaw, WA 98022) functions only as book publisher. As such, the ultimate design, content, editorial accuracy, and views expressed or implied in this work are those of the author.

ISBN 13: 978-1-60615-038-2
ISBN 10: 1-60615-038-3
Library of Congress Catalog Card Number: 2009943653

To the Glory of My Lord and Saviour.

Contents

Acknowledgments

First of all, I would like to thank Mehran for his prayers. They were the keys that opened the gates of heaven for me. Next, I must thank Pastor Asa Kain for his dedication in discipling me. I am also indebted to Pastor Owen Scott for his love, encouragement, and desire to see me fulfill my call. For his fatherly care and method of mentoring, so reminiscent of the apostle Paul, I would like to thank Pastor Patrick Safarian. To the love of my life, Mellissa, who, besides the Lord, is my greatest daily support: thank you for your tireless dedication. I could never have become the man of God that I am without your daily sacrifice and encouragement. No matter how great my conversion to Christ, or how many great men of God mentored me, without my helpmate, I would never have embarked on such a great journey. I would also like to thank the team at iamthirsty.ca for their prayers and support. Last but not least, I need to thank Dan, who has tirelessly helped me to put my thoughts on paper and his wife, Kathy, for all the sacrifices she has made.

Foreword

It is with pleasure and great affection that I write the foreword of this book. This is the story of my spiritual son, Afshin Javid, who has a great love for the Lord Jesus Christ and an enormous passion to reach people of all nations with the message of the Gospel.

During the eight years I have known him, Afshin and I have worked side by side to share God's love with people of many cultures. He and his wife, Mellissa, are truly a gift of God to his people. Together they have three children, who young as they are, share their parents' love and passion for the Lord. I have personally seen how Afshin has grown in his love and devotion for God and has been obedient to the heavenly call on his life. Several years ago, as a step of faith, Afshin and Mellissa dedicated their lives to a full-time ministry after choosing to close a successful business. The Lord has rewarded their dedication with a special anointing and has expanded their territory as never before.

Afshin possesses many godly characteristics, but the one that stands out to me most is his obedience to his immediate Church authorities—a commitment few pastors observe with such seriousness. In 1 Samuel 15:22, God told the prophet Samuel that he preferred obedience over sacrifice. The key to success as a believer is obedience to the Lord's commands, and Afshin lives this. In life, such dedication to Christ pays off. Interestingly, the submission that Afshin has sown in his own life, he now reaps also from his parishioners (see Gal. 6:7). His household and God's household are under his care—dedicated and submissive to him in a healthy and biblical manner.

Afshin's is the life story of a boy God set apart before he was even formed in his mother's womb. His early life was full of zeal but devoid of wisdom. He was full of thirst but tried to quench it at a fountain of death. Then one day he met Jesus and all of this changed. His desire to know God's righteousness has led him into many unpleasant and difficult circumstances, but all of that desire to *seek* God flowed out of being first sought *by* God! Afshin responded to the Lord as his Shepherd and has followed him ever since. He considers all the trials and tribulations to be a source of joy because he knows that in this crucible, he is formed into the image of his divine love, Jesus Christ. He has the full support of his dedicated wife, which is what makes it possible for him to follow the Lord so successfully.

To the reader, Afshin's story might come across as the only story of its kind. But many Iranians are meeting God in a similar way in these last days. God used Persian kings to restore Israel to its own land in the Old Testament. Isaiah prophesied about the great King Cyrus, the founder of the Persian Empire, 150 years before his birth. This king was God's instrument to set his people free from captivity in Babylonia. Cyrus is called God's "shepherd" and his "anointed" to carry on God's purposes on earth (Isa. 44:28–45:3). Interestingly, Afshin named his son Kurosh, the Persian translation of Cyrus.

In modern days, God's faithfulness can be seen in the salvation of Iranians—the descendents of those who helped emancipate his own people twenty-five centuries ago. God is executing the plan he outlines in Jeremiah 49:39. His desire is to set his throne in the hearts of his beloved Muslim people and, at this time, he is accomplishing this with unprecedented haste.

Afshin's story is an eye-opener, showing us that when we are wholly committed to God, he will be with us in any circumstance to which he calls us. If you are not yet a believer, I ask you to pray sincerely as you read this story and ask God to talk to you in a personal way. Ask him to show you the truth. If you are a believer, do not merely marvel at the story and go on your way as if you are not likewise responsible for reaching the lost. Consider the fact that the mission field is no longer beyond the Western borders. People of every tongue, tribe, and nation have come to our door step. Step out of your comfort zone and become an effective citizen of God's kingdom.

It is a great joy for me to recommend this book to you.

Yours in reaching a world in need,
Rev Dr. Patrick Safarian, Pastor
Iranian Christian Church in Seattle

CHAPTER 1

The Silhouette of a Man

The phone rang late in the morning. Mom did the talking. Although my brother Bobby had done all the prior negotiations, it was only 11:00 AM, so naturally he was still asleep. Seiavash was on the other end of the line—our human smuggler—the man we hoped would take us to the United States in exchange for the small fortune we had saved over the past two years. There was urgency in his voice. "You and your family need to pack up your things immediately. We are leaving Pakistan tonight. I will meet you at the airport this afternoon around 3:00 PM. Make sure to pack light—one small bag for each person, *at most*. Your forged passports, tickets, and everything else you'll need will be ready for you. See you then. Don't be late. We can't wait for you."

We had been planning this for such a long time, and finally the day had come. At last, we were going to begin our journey to the West. There was no guarantee what country we would eventually call home. We would take what we could get. This is how it works when you are being smuggled.

We all piled into one taxi and headed for the Karachi Airport—my mom, my older brother Bobby, my older sister, my younger twin brothers, and me. We had three small carry-on bags between the six of us. All our worldly possessions had been lost when we fled our home at the beginning of the war, and everything we had accumulated since then we abandoned in Pakistan.

When we arrived, there was a large group of fellow Iranians congregated at the airport entrance, none of whom we had met. Seiavash told us all to wait outside while he went into the airport. He disappeared for about fifteen minutes. When he returned, four or five officials ushered us past every ticket and immigration counter and security check in the airport. We received our falsified Iranian passports, which had already been stamped. No one even asked our names—Seiavash had taken care of everything with bribes. All we had to do was scoot past the regular travellers and onto the plane. We were all grinning, posing for photos, and chatting excitedly about what lay ahead. We would start by travelling to another Asian country, but we didn't even know which one. For me, it did not matter. I was safe on the plane. All I really cared about was that I could eventually fulfil my grandfather's spiritual commission to me: I must go to the West and preach Islam. The West needed to hear the words of Allah from the Koran and about Mohammad, the last and greatest prophet. When I heard where we were going, I thought, *Malaysia? Where is that? Never heard of it.* This was the beginning of an important detour.

I was born in Abadan, a city of about 200,000 people situated in the southwest corner of Iran in the province of Khuzestan. The Persian Gulf lies to the south and to the east is the Iraq border, the closest Iraqi city being Basra. In the summer, with the humidity, this part of Iran can be sweltering. At midday, it was so hot that if you touched the hood of a car or a door handle that had been sitting in the sun, you would instinctively pull your hand back as if you had touched a hot element on the stove. It was here, in this kind of heat, that I was born in the summer of 1972. Abadan was not much to talk about up until the beginning of the 20th century; it only had a few hundred people and nothing substantial in the way of industry. However, it was soon discovered that Abadan sat on a wealth of oil fields, which were rapidly developed, and with that development the population grew. All the families I knew earned their living in the oil industry or its support:

drilling, refining, engineering, management, export, or otherwise. My family was no exception. My father worked in the Abadan oil refinery and my grandfather, likewise, had worked all of his life in the petroleum industry.

My grandfather was one of the heroes of my childhood because of his devotion to his religious faith and his desire to help others. Having become quite rich as a result of his work, he used his wealth to improve the lives of the Iranian people by building orphanages, schools, and mosques. He was extremely devoted to Islam as a religion and way of life, and since one of the five pillars of Islam is "zakat," or charity work, he did this to the fullest. He was well known for his generosity to friends and strangers. Whenever people needed money, they knew that they could go to him for help, and that he would not expect anything in return. Another of the pillars of the Muslim faith is the "hajj," or pilgrimage to Mecca—a city in the west of Saudi Arabia near the coast. Normally, a Muslim will make a pilgrimage to Mecca once in their lifetime if they can reasonably afford to do so. My grandfather, out of his devotion to Islam, made the pilgrimage not once, but three times. The first of these trips took over two months because he walked on foot through the deserts of Iran, Iraq, and Saudi Arabia. It may startle the Western reader to hear that my grandfather had nineteen children, but it should be understood that he had more than one wife. In fact, he had four wives. This was allowable from both a religious and legal perspective in Iran and, in fact, remains so to this day. I am uncertain of how many first cousins I had, but our family used to joke that half of the city of Abadan was related to us in one manner or another. Sometimes I think this was not an exaggeration. After all, my grandfather had four brothers!

My earliest recollections of my father were of the two of us delivering political flyers door-to-door in our neighbourhood in the evening after dark. My father was very much opposed to the regime of Shah Mohammad Reza Pahlavi, who had reigned in Iran since 1941. The Shah was seen to have systematically undermined traditional Islamic beliefs by attempting to modernize and secularize Iran with economic and social reforms of a decidedly Western bent. For this reason, he was viewed as an enemy to Islam and, since my family was so religious, the Shah was our enemy too. So, we delivered flyers to promote my father's own local political nominations, as propaganda against the Shah and, most importantly, calling for the establishment of an Islamic republic in Iran under the leadership of Ayatollah Ruhollah Khomeini, who would ultimately lead the Islamic revolution. Even at my young age, my father's defiance toward the Shah and his desire for reform was obvious to me, but it was not just my father whom I noticed. Nearly everyone I knew had a similar view. I remember being carried on my dad's shoulders in the streets while mobs shouted, "Death to the Shah! Down with the Shah!" and, "Peace and prosperity be to Khomeini!" It was not surprising, therefore, that my father and my family members were threatened by the soldiers of the Shah's regime.

Once, while on my father's shoulders, he was being encouraged by the wrong end of a rifle to go back into our house and end his demonstrations or be shot. My father, without a second thought, snapped, "Go ahead and shoot me." Fortunately, we did not die that day, but my father's defiance and that of the Iranian people was evident to me. I was being tutored, by example, in this way of thinking and to this level of devotion to Islam. Particularly important was the sense that my grandfather, our patriarch of Islam, was the blessing over, and inspiration for, our devotion to Allah.

Most Iranians in my region had developed an amazing love and passion for Islam, not simply as a religion, but as a way of life, a political ideology and an all encompassing philosophy. Every area of our life was viewed through the lens of the Koran and of the prophet Mohammad. Among Muslims, my family was notable for its fervent devotion. For example, around the time when I was born, I suffered an illness that appeared life threatening. My mother and father pledged that if I survived, I would be dedicated to Imam Reza—the 8th imam of Shia Islam. Because I survived, my hair was not cut until I was five years old, at which time our family made a pilgrimage to the shrine of Imam Reza in the city Mashhad in Iran. There my head was shaved, my hair was weighed, and my parents donated a weight of gold equal to the weight of my hair to the shrine. Such was our devotion to Allah. Since the Shah did not respect Islam, we were at war with him and those who supported him. We were in a holy war for our culture, our faith, and our God.

The Shah's reign ended on February 11, 1979. The day he left Iran, everyone shouted and celebrated the way people always do when they place their hopes in a new political regime, that is before their hopes are dashed by realities. People were lifting their car windshield wiper blades and attaching little white flags and little Iranian flags to the ends of them and then turning them on. People danced on the tops of their vehicles while they inched through the streets, holding up the newspaper headlines which read, "Shah Raft!" that is, "The Shah Has Left!" The atmosphere was absolutely jubilant. We placed all of our hopes on Khomeini, who shortly thereafter established the Islamic Republic of Iran.

My next vivid memories were of the Iran-Iraq war, which started the fall after I turned eight years old. Some of the neighbourhood children and I were playing outside, as we often did, in the centre of a roundabout. A jet seemed to appear out of nowhere, flying low enough that it felt like we could reach up and touch the exhaust trail. A few seconds later we heard a thunderous explosion and the ground shook beneath our feet. Unlike children in the West, who have the great fortune of being politically oblivious, it did not take us long to understand what was happening—the Iraqis were attacking us. Since Abadan is a border city, it would only take hours before tanks began rolling in. My father got into the car with my mother, picked up my four siblings and me, and we fled Abadan with only the clothes on our backs. Everything, whether of sentimental or monetary value, was gone, but my parents were just relieved that we all escaped safely. Unlike them, I remember being confused about why we had to leave so quickly, and why everything had to be left behind. I did not fully understand war, but I did understand our lives were in immediate danger. We had to go and we had to go without delay.

We went to a city called Mahshahr, a ninety-minute drive from Abadan, to stay with my aunt. The general opinion of people was that the war with Iraq would be over within a few days, but one week turned to four and one month turned to three, and soon it was clear that the war with Iraq was going to drag out. Not wanting to wear out our welcome at my aunt's house, we moved to Shiraz, where my grandfather owned property and a house. There we stayed with my father's brother and his children and another of my aunts and her many children. My grandfather was there also with some of his own unmarried children, along with another uncle and his wife. In all, about fifty of us were crammed into a house with eight small rooms. Every square inch of the building became a bedroom—we were all piled on top of one another. In those days, televisions were often raised on four legs. The only space for me to sleep was under that television. I wiggled under it every night. During the day there was no place to sit and we had only one toilet. I remember standing in line in the morning for my opportunity to use the washroom. That's why I laugh now when a family of four can't seem to function without three bathrooms. That being said, I won't pretend we were terribly happy with our living circumstance because this was all quite a change for us.

Growing up, I was a high energy kid—always rambunctious and always getting into trouble. If there was a wall, I wanted to climb it, and if there was a tree, I was going to get to the top branch. When I rode my bicycle, I made jumps in an attempt to land as far away from the takeoff point as humanly possible. As a result, accidents and injuries were my constant companions, but there was something very peculiar about those moments when I was in danger. Out of the corner of my eye, just at the time when I was about to fall or hit my head, there was a silhouette of a tall man standing in the distance. His figure and appearance were not distinct. Whoever he was, I sensed that he was looking out for me and protecting me. When he was there, I knew in my heart everything was going to be okay.

So often and reliably did he appear at these times that I began to tell my family about him. I spoke openly about the man who was looking after me. My grandfather knew that this must be a spiritual man, and concluded that it was Imam Ali, who is the first imam of the Shiite Muslims and the fourth caliph of the Sunni Muslims. Imam Ali is respected by all Muslims, whatever their school of belief, and since we were Shiites, Ali was second only to Mohammad in spiritual importance. Therefore, I developed a great love for the name of Ali because I believed that he himself was my spiritual mentor and protector. As Shiites, we viewed Imam Ali as a symbol of justice, righteousness, and ever-present help, and so he held a position of honour in our hearts and minds. For me, especially, his name was precious. At that time, my knowledge of Islam was shallow and my knowledge of the Koran was also scarce. One thing I had learned from watching the revolution unfold, from hearing the devotion to Islam in the words of my family, and from my grandfather's interpretation of the man who protected me: the study of Islam was important above all human endeavours. Islam was everything. It was all anyone who lived around me cared for, spoke of, and thought about. Because of that, I had to make Islam my everything also.

The new government of Iran facilitated my desire to learn Islam by filling the radio and television broadcasts with teachings of the Koran. Any time we turned on television we found Islamic teaching. In the schools, education in the theology of Islam was treated as more central to our learning than "core" subjects like language and mathematics. As you walked in the streets by the mosques, you would hear the Koran being recited and taught. We were inundated with this teaching, but for us the change was welcome. I remember being happiest when I could watch television or listen to an imam to hear the teachings of the Koran. When the call to prayer was played over loud speakers from the local mosques three times each day, I was mesmerized.

The more I learned of the Koran, the more my conviction grew that the war with Iraq was not political: it was a jihad, a holy war against infidels who had aligned themselves with, and received help from, the United States, the Soviet Union, and the United Kingdom. We believed that because of our devotion to Islam, we were being persecuted by countries all over the globe. We did not see ourselves as aggressors in any way in this conflict. Prior to the revolution, we enjoyed good relations with the West and now, simply because of our religious convictions, we had come under attack. So, it was a jihad and that's how we responded.

There were, of course, people whose convictions did not run as naturally deep as our own. But in this environment people who vocalized a differing opinion did not live long. When Khomeini came to power he made it clear that you were either *for* Islam and the Islamic Republic or you were *against* Islam. If you were against Islam and you let anyone know it, you would be imprisoned and executed. This is why so many people, particularly the educated, fled Iran around this time.

I came to the conclusion that my run-of-the-mill devotion to Allah was not good enough. I needed to understand more and be more. I needed to do more for Allah. He was the great God. There was none beside him. After all, it was only fair. He had sent Imam Ali to save me from injury so many times. How could I withhold anything from Allah since he had done so much for me?

Anything but complete devotion was unthinkable to me. My zeal caught my grandfather's attention. As my devotion for Allah grew, so did the attention and love my grandfather gave me. So, my love for Islam was constantly encouraged and reinforced. I could not help but think I was doing something great—something so significant that my grandfather paid that much attention to me. This drove me to further study and action. At age twelve, my grandfather gave me a beautiful prayer mat, and as Shiite Muslims we had a prayer stone that we placed on the ground and touched with our foreheads as we bowed. The distinction of the devoted man of prayer was for a mark to develop on his forehead from contact with the stone. My grandfather also gave me a set of prayer beads that would help me count the number of times that I had recited my statements of faith or scriptures from the Koran during times of prayer. At least three times a day I would pick up my prayer beads saying, "In the name of Allah who is merciful and gracious." Then I would recite, "Praise be to Allah" thirty-three times and then say, "Peace be upon Mohammad and all his descendants." I would then repeat the cycle of thirty-three plus one another two times. Finally, I would finish with "May Allah protect me from Satan" as I set the beads down. Likewise, as I grew to know more of the Koran by heart, I would often recite a given Surah and then I would repeat it over and over again during my times of prayer. My prayers to Allah were not conversational—they were repetitive and it was by this discipline that I was proving my devotion to him.

When I was twelve years old, I concluded that I was not doing enough for Allah. I needed to show him more convincingly that I loved him. I didn't want there to be any doubt about my devotion to him. I believed I should be willing to risk my life and, if necessary, give it up entirely. To accomplish this I joined the Basij, a volunteer militia established by Khomeini, which was often locally directed by clerics at the neighbourhood mosque.

The goal of the Basij was to see that Islam was followed at every level in our country: the cities, the towns, and the countryside. We in the Basij would also volunteer to go to the front line to fight the infidels, that is, the Iraqis. I was a member of the Basij for about three years.

At that time we commonly referred to any person who supported the Islamic Republic of Iran as members of Hezbollah, which translates, "The Party of Allah." So, as members of Basij, we thought of ourselves as the elite of Hezbollah. People in the West now use the term Hezbollah to refer to a political entity in Lebanon, but this is not how *we* used this term. To us, "Hezbollah" was just a synonym for the Basij.

I kept many of my activities hidden from my family because I knew that not all of my relatives would support my involvement on account of my young age. At fourteen I went one step further: I volunteered to go to the front line in the war with the Iraqis. As front line volunteers, our assignment was a death sentence. We were to run ahead of the official Iranian army through a desert infested with mines. My death was almost a certainty, but I believed that in martyrdom, my trip to heaven was virtually assured. In addition, I was told by my recruiters that if I went to heaven, I would be able to choose seventy family members to join me there. I considered it all worthwhile: I was exchanging my life for a trip to heaven for me and my family.

Boys who were less than fifteen years of age, like me, were required to provide signed consent from their father stating that they were allowed to go to the front line. This was not the sort of waiver a parent signs when they send their child to summer camp. It was a written consent for the child to expend his life in the way of Allah. Knowing that my parents would not give this consent, I lied and said they were both dead. This was quite plausible because they knew I was from the border city of Abadan, and many children from this city had been orphaned by the war. So, the matter was not investigated further and I was accepted to go to the front line without family permission.

On the day we were to travel to the front line, all the other young men and myself piled into several buses. I don't know if the others were scared, but they did not act that way and certainly I was not afraid—this was my destiny. I loved Allah so much and I was going to show him. My father loved me too though, and when he found out what I had done through the rumour mill, he got up at 4:00 AM and drove frantically for two-and-a-half hours to where we were gathered, promptly blowing my cover to the army authorities. He yanked me off the bus. There is no doubt in my mind that most of those other young men died shortly thereafter. In honour of our sacrifice for our country, those who had volunteered for the front line received a special issue Koran from the Iranian government. I got to keep mine in spite of the fact that my mission was aborted, and I have it to this day. Even though I didn't make the trip, there was no doubt in the minds of army officials and members of the Basij about my devotion to the cause.

Having missed out on my opportunity for martyrdom, my grandfather came up with an alternative and potentially more productive plan for my life. He suggested I immigrate to the United States and share Islam with Westerners and bring them to the knowledge of the one true God. I could tell them Islam was the best religion and their best hope to go to heaven. Furthermore, many of my relatives had already immigrated to the U.S. and had come under the influence of Western thinking. I could serve as a touchstone to remind them of where they came from, the value of the true faith of Islam, and the devotion required to be a good Muslim. With this as my new mission, I left Iran in 1987. First I flew to the border city of Zahedan. There I arranged for a human smuggler to accompany me across the border. I travelled on foot. After bribing some border patrol agents in Pakistan, I walked to a small Pakistani village and then paid to be driven to the city of Quetta. From there, I rode a train to Karachi through deserted and mountainous parts of the country. Shortly thereafter, I met up with my brother, Bobby, who was already living in Karachi. He wanted to immigrate to the U.S. also, but his motivation was not religious—he simply wanted a better life.

When I arrived in Karachi, wanting to know all I could about my faith, I decided I needed to learn about Sunni Islam, which holds to the same basic principles of Shia Islam but differs substantially on a number of theological points. Loosely speaking, and I mean *very* loosely speaking, one might think of the division between the Sunnis and Shias to be analogous to the division between the Roman Catholics and the Protestants in that there are two major arms of the faith that differ theologically. I wanted to understand the way the Sunnis thought and why they did things the way they did. So, I sought their tutelage in theology.

At the same time, I became involved with Shiites there and I attended the Hussainia, which is a congregational hall devoted to the remembrance of Husayn Ibn Ali—a Shia imam who was the son of Ali and the grandson of Mohammad. This was a place where we could gather, share our food, and observe various rituals. The most important of these is called the Mourning of Muharram, which marks the death of Imam Husayn in the Battle of Karbala, and occurs each year in the first month of the Islamic calendar. In this ritual, mourners beat their chests with their hands and their backs with a bundle of chains designed for flagellation. The self-inflicted beatings are so prolonged that the backs of the mourners are often covered in blood afterwards.

Meanwhile, my brother and I were trying to figure out a way to get to the United States, Canada, or possibly Europe. The process of arranging illegal migration to the West was not quick—it took us just over two years. During this time, my mother and three other siblings had joined us in Karachi so we could all try to get to North America together. Bobby had made contact with a "reputable" human smuggler, who would assist us in the complex process of obtaining suitable false identification, arranging of flights, itinerary, and bribes of Customs and Immigration, and other logistical details. There were many people in Pakistan who would take your money to smuggle you, but only a few reliably delivered. We had found someone who had a good track record. His name was Seiavash and his price was steep. He wanted $2,000 per person. All other expenses would be *our* problem, with the exception of a modest daily food allowance that he would issue to us. We did not have that kind of money, but fortunately my father had obtained a travel visa to the U.S. and was working under the table at a gas station owned by an old friend now living in California. Gradually, by putting in sixteen-hour work days, he earned the money we needed. On November 14, 1989, after more than two years of planning, we were finally ready to leave Pakistan.

Chapter 2

Locked Up in Kuala Lumpur

It was early evening in Karachi and we had gathered at the airport for the flight that I would soon discover was headed for Kuala Lumpur. Our group included my mother, my four siblings, and a number of other Iranians also seeking to immigrate to Europe or North America. Between all of the various parties, we were a group of about thirty.

None of us had legal Iranian passports because none of us had previously travelled abroad, and, on account of the war, the government was not issuing any new ones. Obviously, if there was a mass exodus, Iran would be defeated. So we were all given falsified Iranian passports by our smuggler. In addition, each of us received a second falsified passport, but this time from a Western country. All of the Western passports were stolen and bore the name of some poor, hapless tourist. In those days, passport fraud was, in fact, very straightforward as Seiavash would later show me. Few counties used sophisticated security features on their passports and, to make our job easier, some did not even bother to laminate the photo to the paper. Literally, all we had to do was lift the existing photo with a razor blade and then glue a photo of someone else's face into the empty space. Beyond using stolen passports to attempt immigration, as far as I am aware, nobody in our group was involved in any other illegal activities. We were all simply seeking a better life in the West.

In the Karachi airport we were ushered right onto the airplane. Leaving Pakistan, we used the Iranian passports, but while we were in the air, we all switched to those from various Western countries. These Western passports would allow us to travel into Europe, Canada, or the U.S. Once we arrived in our destination country, we could secretly dispose of the passport and claim refugee status with no documents and no paper trail. The passport I used to land in Malaysia was Dutch. From that point on, I would be answering to the name "Mr. Haringes."

By the time we arrived in Kuala Lumpur, I had run out of cash. I could not speak any English, just Farsi. I could read some Arabic because of my studying of the Koran, but the language of the Koran is so different from modern, spoken Arabic that it is of little use in communication. The only Dutch words I knew were "goede nacht" ("good evening") and I was going to milk these two words for all they were worth.

Unfortunately for me, it was morning when we arrived in Malaysia. As I approached the customs and immigration desk, the officer began to ask me all kinds of questions, presumably in English, but I had no idea what he was saying. I just kept politely responding, "Goede nacht." He seemed a little frustrated, but persisted. When he started rubbing his fingers together, I knew from the context that he was trying to ask me how much cash I was carrying—a common question at border crossings. If I told him that I had no money, it would immediately arouse suspicion. Furthermore, it was pretty obvious that there was something fishy about a Middle Eastern teenager going by the last name "Haringes," who could only say "good night," and was saying it in the morning. So, I needed a distraction from his question about money.

I called to a group of strangers who happened to be passing behind the immigration counter on their way to the boarding area. "Hey! Hey!" I yelled, excitedly waving with a big smile on my face. One guy happened to turn around to see where all the noise was coming from and, seeing me waving at him, thought I was someone he had met before but did not recognize. He timidly waved back with a confused look, as you sometimes do to avoid the embarrassment of admitting that you have forgotten someone's face. I pointed to my new acquaintance and joyfully announced "Friend! Friend!"—one of my few English words. The officer, apparently not wanting to be bothered trying to extract any more answers from this nutcase of a Dutch kid, stamped my passport and ushered me on. Bobby also managed to get by his officer, as did my whole family.

Gathering at the front of the airport with the rest of the Iranians who had managed to squeeze past immigration, we headed into the centre of the city to look for a hotel. We ended up in Jalan Sultan, the Chinatown of Kuala Lumpur, and rented hotel rooms. Our hotel was called the Nan Yeang, located at No. 83 Jalan Sultan 50000. We stayed in room number 301. Our food budget, as doled out by Seiavash, was about six Malaysian ringgit (their unit of currency) per meal, but when I strolled through Chinatown I was not sure how I was going to buy anything to eat because all of the foods were so bizarre to me: octopus, chicken feet, and other things I would have previously dismissed as inedible. So we sourced out various American fast-food chains and that's where we ate, but the prices were burning up our budget and the American food was not something we were used to. As Iranians, we wanted a meal with bread or rice and meat and vegetables. I decided to go on a quest to find some better food.

I walked northeast for about an hour and ended up in Little India, where I felt much more comfortable. The foods they were selling were similar to what I had eaten in Pakistan, and the people there spoke Hindi, which was very close to the Pakistani language of Urdu. I approached a street vendor who was selling donair kebabs in small hotdog buns for two ringgit. It was a decent meal and it was much cheaper than American fast food. Then I got a bright idea as to how I could make a little pocket money. Under our hotel there was a bakery which sold baguettes. I went and bought a big baguette for one ringgit, and then I headed back to the kebab vendor and ask him to fill this larger baguette with meat, which cost me two ringgit. I went back to the hotel, sliced my baguette sandwich into thirds, put it all on a plate in the common area, and waited. The bait worked: all of the other Iranians were drooling over my meal. "Hey man, that looks delicious. Where did you get it?"

"Oh, I had to walk something like six or eight miles into Little India to get this kind of food. It was so far," I said. The truth was, I had only walked about two miles.

"Wow, that's too far to go for one meal," they said. "How much did it cost?"

"It was only three ringgit per sandwich," I said.

"That's so cheap! Are you going back tomorrow?"

"Yes, I can pick you guys up some sandwiches if you want. No problem."

"Please do. That would be great!"

After that, I made a daily trek to Little India and pocketed six ringgit for every baguette I bought, filled with meat, and sold. With the money I made, I bought a hot plate and cookware and started a little makeshift Iranian cafeteria out of my room, selling meals for six ringgit each. My mother got in on the business, doing a lot of the cooking and this is how I made my living in Kuala Lumpur.

Seiavash noticed how industrious and organized I was and he brought me under his wing for some of the preparations for our group to leave Malaysia. For example, he taught me how to forge passports and how the human smuggling business worked. Eventually, he grew to trust me and commissioned me to look after our group's illegal passports.

Not all of our friends and family travelled to their ultimate destinations together out of Malaysia, and by no means did all of them go to North America. Many went to European countries. As it happened, my mother and three of my siblings got their opportunity to leave Malaysia before Bobby and I did. Over the next few days they would successfully migrate to Canada, while Bobby and I remained in Kuala Lumpur. Our smuggler assured us that our opportunity would come in about two weeks, so we had no choice but to wait.

I remember coming home fairly late one night, shortly after my mother and three siblings had left for Canada. I was so tired, and I just wanted to go to bed. However, I was feeling strangely uneasy. One of the other Iranians, Amir, who had stayed in our hotel with his family, had just left, and I knew he was a little shifty. I could not trust him. I was worried that once he had parted our company, he might betray us in some way. So, despite being tired, I left the hotel I was in, rented a room in a different hotel, and took the thirty illegal passports with me. By this time it was about 2:30 AM, and I was dead tired. However, even though I had gone to the trouble of changing hotels, for some reason I felt compelled to return to the place where we had all been staying. Defying all reason, I got up and walked back. I didn't even know why. It later became clear that God was the author of this decision.

Because I was feeling so twitchy and I did not want to get caught with them, I left the illegal passports locked in the room of the other hotel. I could pick them up in the morning when I felt calmer. When I finally got back to my original hotel room, having abandoned my plan to sleep elsewhere, it was 4:00 or 5:00 AM. At about 7:00 AM there was a pounding on the door. Immigration officers and police barged into our room, demanding our identification. We had indeed been betrayed. There were three of us in the room: Bobby, me, and a friend of ours named Fariborz, who had been rooming with us. We knew that the best thing for us to do was to admit we were illegal migrants and claim we had no documents. Fortunately, all of the illegal passports were at the other hotel so a search would reveal nothing. If they had been found in our room, we would have been charged with human smuggling, which was a much greater crime than illegal migration. Bobby, Fariborz and I were arrested there in the hotel room. The date was January 15, 1990.

As it happened there was another young man, Mehran, from an aristocratic background, who was in our company but staying in another room in the hotel. His father had been an Iranian diplomat stationed in France during the reign of the Shah. He did not even look ethnically Iranian, and having been educated in a French private school, he was completely fluent in French and English. By what appeared to be a very unfortunate fluke, Mehran and another friend of ours named Saeed dropped by our room while the police and immigration officers were arresting us. They pushed open the door and marched right into the drama that Bobby, Fariborz, and I had found ourselves in. Immediately the officials began questioning Mehran and Saeed about their relationship to us. Of all the people we knew, Mehran, because of his appearance and fluency in other languages, was in the best position to try to save his own skin. But he caved immediately and admitted he was

Iranian, so he and Saeed were also nabbed. All five of us were thrown into a temporary lockup in Kuala Lumpur—about a five-minute drive from the hotel.

We were terrified because we did not know what was going to become of us. Furthermore, because we used forged IDs, there was no trail of evidence that we had travelled from Pakistan to Malaysia. Not even our families could help us because they had no idea where we were—neither did the Iranian government. Furthermore, we were not allowed to make any phone calls.

Mehran was completely dejected. "You know why we are here, guys?"

"Because that worthless idiot, Amir, ratted us out to the police," I said. "When I get out of here, I am going to hunt him down and kill him."

"No, Afshin, it is not because of Amir. It is because of God. God has brought us here to straighten us out."

I exploded.

"Are *you* trying to lecture *me* about *God?* I am the one who prays every day. I am the one who knows the Koran backwards and forwards. I am the one who was in the Basij, and *you* are trying to tell *me* something about God—*you* who I have never seen praying?"

"Oh, no, Afshin, I am not talking about *that* God," he said. "I am not talking about Allah."

This simply did not compute. What was he talking about? There is only one God, Allah—the same one that the Jews and Christians worship, but they are all mixed up about his commands.

"Okay, Mehran, what God are *you* talking about then?" I was sitting on the floor, but at this point I repositioned my legs so I could lunge at him if he said anything other than "Allah."

"I am talking about Jesus . . ." As I heard that word, there was an immediate and almost audible rebuttal in my head. I heard a voice say, "*La ilaha illa Allah*," which means, "There is no god but Allah."

I didn't even let him finish the sentence before I sprang from the floor and pulled my arm back to punch him. But Bobby grabbed me before I could reach him and scolded Mehran for agitating me.

"Are you crazy, trying to pick a fight with this guy, Mehran? Afshin thinks that even *I* am an infidel, and *I* am a Muslim! If I am an infidel in Afshin's eyes, then rest assured, you are much worse off. If you want to live to see the light of day, I would not mess with Afshin about religion."

I resolved in my mind that I should kill Mehran for his blasphemy, but eventually I settled down and just planned ways that I could humiliate him for his beliefs. The problem was that I had no idea what Christians believed, so I did not know where to start. I had never seen their holy book and I had never really had a conversation with any of them. In the end, I decided just to intimidate Mehran whenever possible.

A day or two later, we woke up in the early morning to the moaning and groaning of a fellow prisoner. The lock-up was laid out in such a way that there were cells forming a square, and in the centre of the square, there was another cell where prisoners could be put on display for punishment. This poor soul was in the centre cell, on the floor, writhing, sweating, and shaking. We found out from the others that he was a drug addict and needed medical attention for withdrawal, and probably a number of other things, but the guards and officials totally ignored him all that day. His howling was disturbing. As the hours went by, he gradually began to produce foam from his mouth, and he had ongoing fits of violent shaking. After about ten hours, he died right there in the centre cell. The guards came, confirmed his death, and removed his body.

We realized at this point that we were in a country where prisoners had no rights and where rules and regulations, and even a human life, did not seem to matter too much. I turned to Bobby. "Look, Bobby, if we die here, no one is going to find out about it. Somehow we need to get the message out to our family that we are stuck in here so that if we die, at the very least, our parents will know and there is a chance someone will be held accountable." With no evidence that we had even entered the country, denying what had happened to us would be very easy for the Malaysian government.

"I don't know, Afshin. There is really nothing we can do right now. Why, you got any ideas?"

"I can make myself sick, and maybe they will take me to see a doctor, and I can get a message out to Mom and Dad somehow."

"What are you talking about? What do you mean, you can make yourself sick?"

"I will show you, Bobby. Believe me, I can do this."

At this point, I turned to a practice I learned about in my time studying Shia Islam and through my meditation in the Koran: I would call upon the Jinn. Westerners are at least casually familiar with the notion of contacting the supernatural realm by means of séances, meditative techniques, Ouija boards, and magical spells. The concept of interaction with the spirit realm is present and, in fact, well-known in Islam.

Muslims believe in the existence of a parallel race of spirit beings referred to as the Jinn, from which the English word "Genie" is derived. The Jinn are not considered equivalent to angels and demons but are lesser spirit beings. The Koran frequently discusses the Jinn, indicating they are made from fire,[1] as opposed to humans, who are formed from clay.[2] The Koran also has many verses in which Mohammad addresses the Jinn directly with exhortations beginning, "O you assembly of Jinns and men."[3] Muslims believe that the Jinn, like us, have the choice to be religious or not and can decide, therefore, to be Muslim or not.

Although there is an entire Surah (chapter) of the Koran named after the Jinn, many of the Muslim beliefs about them do not come from the Koran itself but from a collection of writings referred to as the Hadith. These are stories of the prophet Mohammad: things he said, things he did, and general advice for living, conduct, and justice. Many of the Muslim religious traditions and beliefs are derived from these writings. The Hadith are thought to have been recorded by contemporary followers of Mohammad and subsequently evaluated for their authenticity and compiled. Not all Hadith are considered legitimate ("canonical") by all Muslims, but most would acknowledge that the collections assembled by Sahih Bukhari and Sahih Muslim are trustworthy. The first biography of Mohammad, *Sirat Rasul Allah* or *The Life of Allah's Messenger*, written by Ibn Ishaq, is also given widespread credibility. In addition, the Hadith is the source of much of the interpretation of the Koran itself because the Koran is not really a document that can be understood without commentary. Unlike the Bible, which has history, narratives, poetry, prophecy, and exhortation, and is comprehensible in isolation, the Koran is mostly exhortation but without contextual information. The Hadith adds essential historical and narrative context to the Koran. When stories do appear in the Koran, they are often derived from biblical narratives but with notable modifications, often of enormous theological significance.

Contact with the Jinn is discouraged for those who have inadequate religious education and is generally viewed more negatively by Sunni Muslims than Shia Muslims. However, as a devout Shia Muslim, to my mind I was not forbidden from communicating with the Jinn. In fact, there are Hadith that indicate that Mohammad did the same. It is very clear from both the Koran and Hadith that Mohammad and the early Muslims believed that the Jinn listen to the recitation of the Koran[4] and I had been taught that Mohammad had personally instructed the Jinn.

My contact with the Jinn occurred as a direct result of meditation in the scriptures of the Koran. To be more specific, in the Koran there are certain Surahs which begin with sets of Arabic letters having no apparent meaning. These are referred to as the "Secrets" or the "Mysterious Letters" of the Koran. Although there is a great deal of hypothesis, no one really knows the meaning or purpose of these letters. I had begun meditative chanting of the Secrets of the Koran some time earlier, and by this means I had developed frequent communication with the Jinn. I had learned the practice of calling on them in order to make something happen—either for a favour for me or a friend, or payback to an enemy for wrong done to me.

In the lockup in Kuala Lumpur, I called on the Jinn again. I prayed sickness over myself. Within a short time, I developed an incredible fever and since I was not an addict, was previously healthy, and was quite a young man, the prison staff did take pity on me and sent me to a local hospital under guard. While travelling to the hospital, I engaged the guard in a conversation and convinced him that if we could drop by a hotel where one of my friends was staying, I could provide him a bribe. That way I could tell my friends where we were and they could, in turn, let my parents and family know what was going on. He agreed. We proceeded to the hospital, where I received an intravenous and some medication, and then we went to my friend's room at the hotel.

After explaining what happened, my friend paid the guard the bribe and agreed to contact my parents. Then the guard returned me to lockup.

That day in the lockup, there was a particularly annoying guard on duty who was mocking me in front of two other guards. I could not understand him because he was speaking Malay, but I could pick out the words "Iran" and "Iranian" as they were all laughing. I gradually grew more angry. Finally, amidst uproarious laughter I heard him say, "Ayatollah Khomeini, ha ha ha!"

With that, I really lost my temper. *How dare this worthless infidel speak against Khomeini? He has insulted Islam! He has slandered Allah! He's going to find out who he is messing with now!* I prayed a curse on him as I summoned all of my contempt, all of my hatred, all of my violent thoughts, and all of my disgust for this pagan. I gathered all the darkness, all the blackness, and all the poison I could summon into a curse, drew my gaze toward him, fixed my eyes on his, took a deep breath, and blew all that spiritual venom across the room like a spitting cobra.

Suddenly, a look of terror crossed his face. He grabbed his throat and began gasping for air. I maintained eye contact with him and let him suffer for a while. He looked up and flipped his head back and forth as if he were trying to shake himself free. I finally withdrew the prayer and he was able to breathe again. He knew I had been given powers from another realm, and he ran down the hall and never mocked me again.

I understand that a Western reader, even a Western Christian reader, may find these things very difficult to accept as true, but I want to give complete assurance: those spirits are real, their powers are real, and when I asked the Jinn to do something within their power, they were willing to do what I asked.[5] Another thing that needs to be understood is that these powers were obtained by the chanting, recitation, and meditation on the scriptures of the Koran alone and from no other book, teaching, or coaching. After this episode, people became very afraid of me because they had seen these things occur.

The lockup was a filthy, dirty, smelly, hot, and miserable place. However, the greatest misery for us was the bugs that made their homes in the darkness of the cracks in the walls. I am not sure what sort of species they were, but I think they might have been some kind of tick—about a quarter of an inch long. In any case, they gave the most horrible and painful bites which burned terribly and itched and then usually became infected. You could not kill these things with your hands. They were built like tanks and could not be squished. The only way we could kill them reliably was to use their armour against them. When they retreated into the crevices in the wall, we would light a match and insert it into the crack. As the air in the crack heated, they would explode with a little "pop!" In this way, matches became a commodity which could only be obtained by bribery of the guards. Even though we had a defence against these horrible things, they came in unstoppable numbers. Every dark place had hoards of them lurking in its shadows.

One day I removed my shirt and my cellmates were all cringing with disgust, saying, "Afshin, look at your back, man. What a mess! It is all swollen and red. I think your skin is infected." I did not feel well, but I did not know why. My cellmates were so concerned that they brought me to the guards, who were equally horrified by the appearance. Fortunately, they provided me some medication and cleaning supplies so that we could wash up our cell to help prevent this from happening to us again.

We spent about three weeks in the lockup before being transferred to a longer term facility, Penjara Pudu prison, on February 6. Pudu was built in 1895 by the British. It is located near the centre of the city and entered the limelight in 1986 when two Australians, Kevin Barlow and Brian Chambers, were executed for drug trafficking under new, very tough, Malaysian trafficking laws. It is said that Pudu was designed for about 300 prisoners, but by 1984 it was housing more than 2,000. The prison was notorious for its inhumane conditions and the fact that no one had ever escaped.

While we were being processed, we saw what we thought was a female prisoner being strip-searched in a humiliating and degrading fashion. "Take off your shirt!" the guard ordered. She was stripped naked and her breasts were exposed, and when it was clear that there was nothing concealed he said, "Now your pants—take them off!" The prisoner reluctantly complied, and I was shocked to see that the prisoner was actually a man. He must have been involved in some sort of transsexual prostitution. Everything about our initiation at Pudu prison was disturbing. As bad as things had been in the lockup, we had seen nothing compared to the misery that would follow.

CHAPTER 3

The Beginning of My Confusion

After processing, we were strip-searched and handed a half-gallon plastic bucket. This would serve for both washing and eating. We were taken outside and escorted to an above ground tank of water and told to bathe. "You will be given thirty seconds," the guard barked, "ten seconds to wet yourself, ten seconds to soap yourself, and then ten seconds to rinse off." He began his threefold countdown of ten seconds, and we washed ourselves with a bar of soap they had provided. This is how we bathed for the entire duration of our time in Pudu prison.

After our frantic bath, we were marched to our cell. For the first couple of days they put us in Room 2 of Cellblock D, but after this we were moved to Room 80 of the same block. Each cell was about six and a half feet by ten feet and housed all five of us. The walls were concrete, and the solid wood door was about two and a half inches thick. There was a narrow slit positioned at eye level so the guards could see in. In each cell, opposite the door, there was a small, arch-shaped window, measuring roughly three feet by two feet. It had vertical bars, and behind the bars were fixed horizontal metal louvers which spanned the width of the prison wall to the outside. Because of the way the louvers were oriented, I could not see the yard unless I pulled myself up to the top of the arch, squeezed my face between the bars, and peeked through the cracks between adjacent louvers. In the corner of the room there was a rubberized bucket with no lid. This was our toilet. Other cells had the good fortune of having a lid for their bucket to control the stench of urine and excrement. We had no such luxury. Our situation was made even worse due to the terrible heat and humidity of Malaysia, from which there was simply no escape.

At 7:00 AM each day, we were ordered out of our cells and lined up in rows while a headcount was performed. While this was taking place, the prison staff would pour us each a small portion of insipid, flavourless rice soup, which was nearly devoid of nourishment. Years later, I saw something similar at a Chinese restaurant and realized that the cooks at Pudu were trying to make a dish called congee. Believe me, the congee in Canada is much better tasting. Since there were no complaint forms at Pudu, and because there was no other food, we ate it. When the headcount was complete we would return to our cells until 10:00 AM, when they would bring us out again, this time for lunch—a small variety of equally unappetizing, flavourless meals.

Free time in the prison yard began at 10:00 AM. At 12:30 PM they gave us dinner. At 1:00 PM we were locked into our cells where we would remain until breakfast. Because of the unusual timing of the meals, we were without food from shortly after noon each day until 7:00 AM the next morning. We were locked up twenty-one hours per day.

The temperature in the cell was typically 95–110 degrees Fahrenheit with 70–90 percent humidity. Of course, there was no air conditioning anywhere in Pudu, nor were there any fans. We slept on the bare concrete and, with five of us in the cell, we had to lie like sardines in a row so that everybody had room. We were given a thin, army-style blanket with a harsh, itchy feel to use for a sleeping mat, to cover ourselves, or as a pillow if we folded it up. We were issued a single 18 x 12 inch towel. My worldly possessions consisted of a pair of shorts, one T-shirt, my towel, and my blanket. Life was miserable and the treatment of prisoners was horrendous.

As the days and weeks passed, we learned more about our fellow prisoners. Mehran made the acquaintance of an American[6] who had been imprisoned for possession of marijuana and had been sentenced to death under the Malaysian drug laws. This poor guy was in a state of suspended animation. The United States government was lobbying hard for his release, but the Malaysians, wanting to save face, refused to release him. After a while, the guards moved the American and we assumed he had been executed, although we had no way to confirm this. We owe this man thanks because when he was moved, he gave us the lid to his bucket and our room did not smell as bad after that.

We also met a number of other people who, like us, were in for immigration violations. Many of them were Indonesians and Sri Lankans.

"So, you are in for immigration too?" we asked one such man.

"Yes, I was in the country illegally and was caught without a passport by the police. I was just looking to get some work so I could feed my family. It was a little easier for me to get work here than at home."

"How long have you been in?"

"Close to three years now. You guys just arrived?"

"Yes," I said, "a couple of weeks ago."

"Tell me, how long did you have to wait before you saw a judge?" I asked.

"I haven't seen a judge."

"What do you mean?"

"Just what I said. I have not been before a judge."

"You have been here three years and you have not seen a judge?"

"That's right."

"Well, have they given you a formal charge or given you a sentence even?"

"No."

"So, how long do you expect to be here?"

"I have no idea. You see that guy over there?"

"Yes."

"He's been here seven years. If no one from the outside helps you, you may be here for a long time."

My heart sank. The gravity of our situation was hitting me. We could be stuck in Pudu for years without being charged or sentenced. Imagine what we could have faced if we had been caught with the illegal passports! We were terrified. There did not seem to be any hope for a quick release.

The air in the cell was always hot, humid, and completely still. There was never a breeze, never a gust, nothing to refresh us—just the warm stench of our urine. We always felt as if there was not enough oxygen for the five of us. We would sit motionless for hours, just to feel a little less starved for air. After a couple of months of this, I started unravelling psychologically. I would fantasize about killing my cellmates because then I could at least catch my breath. We all experienced these feelings. I would often lie on the floor of the cell and position my nose under the door so I could catch some of the cooler air that flowed down the hallway. I even remember being thankful that my nose was big.

Sometimes in the morning, before sunrise, we were awakened to the slow, rhythmic pounding of a drum, sounding as if it came from underneath our cells: "Boom . . . boom . . . boom." The vibration of the bass resonated eerily through the concrete. It sounded ominous, but at first we did not know what it meant. It went on for about thirty minutes, and then it was quiet again. We began to ask around about it and we found out that the drums were played during executions. A lot of people were hung for their crimes at Pudu prison, and the drums were intended to scare the spirit of the deceased out of the building so that it would not become haunted. Every time we heard those drums, we knew that another soul was dying in Pudu. We also knew that our lives held no value. They were totally expendable. No one would have compassion on us. We despaired for our future because there was nothing to rest our hope on. All I had was Islam, and I spent most of my time in prayer and meditation.

We had some medical problems in Pudu. For example, I developed a infection on my scalp that caused my skin to break open and constantly ooze yellow fluid. It would also form a crust as it dried out. I am told, from the description, that that this was probably "impetigo," which is usually caused by the bacteria staphylococcus. In the morning, my head would be stuck to the blanket I was using as a pillow. I would have to yank it off, and my hair would come off with it.

Malaysia was about 60% Muslim and the government actively promoted Islam. Many of the guards and officials in the prison were also Muslim. On the day of my arrival at Pudu, I made it known that I was anxious to have a copy of the Koran, which was provided immediately. I read through the Koran once every ten days and I spent hours each day in prayer and meditation. I had already committed two thirds of the Koran to memory and so, even if I did not have the book itself, I could still recite long, uninterrupted sections. Having the book was of course much better. It was holy. That is, I believed that the book itself, the paper and ink, were holy. I would pick up the Koran, kiss it, touch it to my forehead, and embrace it in my chest. We always placed the Koran onto the highest shelf in our homes because it deserved preeminence over all other worldly possessions.

One of the problems I had in prison was that there was no Muslim cleric available to do the call to prayer and to teach at the prison mosque. Issuing the "call to prayer" or *adhan,* as it is called, is not just a matter of ringing a bell or informally gathering your fellow believers. It is a specific, formulaic announcement that is sung over loud speakers, usually from the minaret of a mosque, three times each day for Shiites and five times each day for the Sunnis. The *adhan* differs slightly between the Sunni and the Shia Muslims, but the Shia version is as follows:

Allah is the greatest x 4
I testify that there is no god but Allah x 2
I testify that Mohammad is Allah's Messenger x 2
I bear witness that Ali is the vice regent of Allah x 2
Make haste to prayers x 2
Make haste to deliverance x 2
Make haste to the best act x 2
Allah is the greatest x 2
There is no god but Allah x 2

We were able to go to the prison mosque during our break from 10:00 AM to 1:00 PM. It was not an official mosque, per se. It was really just a meeting area for Muslims to pray and spend time together. Although I would certainly have preferred to do all of the five daily prayers at a real mosque, I was happy that I was able to at least do the noon prayer in this holy place. I brought up my concern about the lack of a formal call to prayer to a guard.

"Why don't we have call to prayer, at least for the noon prayers?" I asked.

"Oh, my brother, no one knows the call to prayer by heart, and for that matter, none of us really knows the Koran and Hadith well enough to teach anyone else."

I was totally perplexed by this. What kind of Muslims were these people that they don't even know the call to prayer?

"No one here knows the call to prayer by heart?" I said.

"No."

"Do you think I can give the call?"

"Of course. Why not?"

From that point on, I was the unofficial *muezzin*, the one who sings the call to prayer. Realizing that there was no teaching happening at the mosque, I started leading informal discussions and teaching Islam to the men who gathered at lunch. There was a big theological problem though: I was Shia, and Malaysians are Sunni. Of course, they knew I was from Iran and was Shia. This would normally have represented a huge barrier. What they could not deny, however, was that I was by far the most devout Muslim either imprisoned or employed at Pudu. My knowledge of Islam and my devotion to the faith were considered prodigious, given my relative youth. (Perhaps my knowledge was not entirely surprising. After all, I had studied Islam to the exclusion of all else for the preceding three years.) So, under the circumstances, my cellmates overlooked my Shia theology and gave me the role as "unofficial official teacher." Out of loyalty, I called the Shia and not the Sunni version of the *adhan* each lunch hour. No one seemed to care. I taught a small but devoted group of about ten people who came for prayer and study each day during free time.

With twenty-one hours available for devotion to Allah, I extended my prayers far beyond what was mandatory for me as a Muslim. Normally, Muslims will do seventeen *rakat* (cycles of prayer) per day: two in the morning, four at noon, four in the afternoon, three at sunset, and four at night. Each cycle is essentially identical, although minor variation is permissible. Each *rakat* is comprised of specific Koranic recitation, prayer, and ritualistic physical demonstrations of devotion such as bowing and prostration. Muslims are required to recite the first Surah of the Koran and often choose to recite the 112th Surah,[7] which is said by some Muslims to be a distillation of their beliefs.

To the mandatory prayers and recitations I would add much longer Surahs, which I had memorized over the years. Between the prayers I would read the Koran more and more, and I would meditate on the regular scriptures and the Secrets, those letters without known meaning. I would repeat the same *aya* over and over in a chant. The term *aya* means "verse" in English, but the Arabic word carries the connotation of miracle or sign. Thus each *aya* is like an individually packaged divine revelation of Allah to Mohammad via Gabriel.

My desire was to have more of the power I had already developed. I needed the power of Allah more than ever. I needed to have his strength to survive the days and weeks in Pudu. I was fully immersed in Islam—eating, sleeping, and breathing the words of the prophet.

The Jinn would communicate with me conversationally. I don't believe that my cellmates could hear what I was hearing, but I heard audible voices when the spirits entered my room. They would request the recitation of the Koran, which was consistent with what was written in both the Koran and Hadith. In return for the favour of recitation, they would increase my spiritual powers. For example, I was able to close my eyes and tell what people were doing elsewhere or to listen to conversations happening in another room. As the powers of the Jinn increased in me, so also did the respect of my Muslim peers. It became apparent to them that I was a means by which they could obtain information that was otherwise out of reach. They would ask me questions, and I could provide accurate information. They would also bring me requests for revenge, which I would oblige by praying curses on their enemies. Others whom I had met before my imprisonment would issue curses by writing an appropriately negative Koranic scripture on a little piece of paper and placing it in their enemies' vicinity or among their possessions. I am not exaggerating when I say that those whom I cursed would, within days, have an accident or get sick. These experiences had made me power hungry, and the jail cell provided me the time I needed to develop my relationship with the Jinn more fully.

Meanwhile, we still wanted to get out of Malaysia, and the Malaysian government was anxious to get rid of us also. It was expensive and inconvenient to keep international prisoners, and they wanted us out of their hair. However, they did not want to release us back onto the streets of Kuala Lumpur. They wanted us out of the country entirely. In fact, they were willing to partake in *any* plan that would get us out of their country, even if it broke the same laws for which we were imprisoned.

Around the same time, my mother and younger siblings had claimed refugee status in Canada and were living in an apartment in Richmond, British Columbia—a suburb of Vancouver. Our Pakistani smuggler, Seiavash, was also in Vancouver. He had come under the suspicion of the Canadian authorities and was trying to lay low to avoid questioning or arrest. He approached my mother and asked her if he could hide out in her apartment for a few days. She was happy to look after him in this way. Because of the kindness my mother showed him, when he made his way back to Malaysia, he felt obliged to help us get out of Pudu prison. So he produced falsified Iranian passports for me, Bobby, and Fariborz and booked us flights to Nepal. He did not help Mehran or Saeed because they had been under the care of a different smuggler. He approached the front desk at Pudu prison and showed them the passports and tickets.

The staff there was more than happy to use these passports and tickets to get rid of us and accepted them gladly. When the day of the flight arrived, they even drove us out to the airport. We were overjoyed but felt so sad for Mehran and Saeed, who had been left behind. We arrived for our flight, but while we were still in the airport under guard, it was brought to our attention that we would need a Thai visa for our stopover in Bangkok. We explained that we were going on to Nepal with no intention to leave the flight in Thailand, but we were flatly refused at all levels. There was nothing we could do. The guards were not free to release us, and we were returned to our cells at Pudu later that day. Freedom had slipped through our fingers. Mehran and Saeed were stunned to see us back with them again. I cannot express the despair I felt in my heart that day.

However, an unusual question had popped into my mind the day of our near release. It didn't make much sense really, but I wanted to know what Christians say and what they think. I knew that Mehran was a Christian, but he was not very devout. Some of his behaviour was actually appalling to me, but I was still interested in what he believed. I made a mental note to take the time to learn what Christians believe when I got to North America. This was not against my Muslim beliefs, because the prophet Mohammad encourages Muslims to consult the *ahl al kitab* ("people of the book"—a generic term for Jews or Christians) if it assists them in their own faith.[8]

While the Koran could not be described as painting a consistently favourable view of Christians and Jews,[9] it was permissible for me to investigate their beliefs. Strangely enough, I had a sudden compulsion to do so.

One night I was praying, reading the Koran, and meditating after my friends had fallen asleep. Through the slit in the door that the guards used to check on us, with a little beam of light shining, I positioned my Koran just right so I could make out the words and study. As I was praying, I felt the presence of a spirit enter the room. This had happened many times before and I had grown accustomed to it. Who would it be this time? Perhaps I would gain another ability. Immediately, however, I recognized that something was different about this spirit: I sensed its intention to kill me. This had never happened in the past. There had always been a friendly give and take between me and the Jinn. I had never felt jeopardized. As the spirit's presence approached me, panic rose within me. I was filled with fear. I did not know what to do. I couldn't move a muscle. I tried everything in my power to send the spirit away. "In the name of Allah, who is merciful and gracious, I command you to depart!" I knew that Satan and evil spirits should be afraid of the name of Allah. To my dismay, the name of Allah had no effect whatsoever.

The spirit drew ever closer. "I believe that God is one! I am a Muslim! I believe in Mohammad the messenger of Allah!" I shouted, to no avail. I recited other scriptures, one after the other in rapid succession, but I felt like I was firing a machine gun full of blanks.

The spirit came closer and closer still. Maybe I could wake up Bobby and the others. Maybe they could help me send this demon away. But as I looked over at them, for some reason they all appeared to be dead.

I despaired that the spirit had already killed them and I was next! I was drowning in my fear. Finally, I felt the spirit physically choking me. In the same manner that I had called the Jinn to hurt others, so also were they attacking me. They had no loyalty but to themselves! Gasping for air, I finally called out in Farsi "Khoda! Komakam kon!" meaning, "God! Help me!"

Suddenly, I heard a voice in my head, as clear and distinct as when someone calls your name.

"Bring the name of Jesus," it said.

Theologically speaking, this made no sense to me as a Muslim, but just as when a man is drowning and someone throws him a rope, he does not question the colour of the rope. He just grabs on for dear life. I did not give it a second thought but immediately cried out in my desperation, "Jesus, if you are true, show me yourself!"

To this day, I do not know why I phrased it that way, but before the sentence was finished, the spirit was gone. Everything had returned to normal. This was not the point of my conversion, but rather the beginning of my confusion.

CHAPTER 4

The Encounter

Why would Jesus help me? Why would Jesus help a Muslim?

I sat there in the dark, completely flabbergasted. It was not as if I did not respect Jesus. The Koran contains many references to Jesus. He was one of the greatest prophets of Allah who ever lived. Although I did not believe that he was the Son of God, I did believe that he was born of the Virgin Mary, that he was a great teacher, and that he did many miracles in his lifetime. Some of us even believed that Jesus led a sinless life. We held that Jesus had ascended to heaven without dying and was with Allah. We also believed he would return and usher in the Day of *Qiyamah*, that is, the Day of Judgement.

So for me, Jesus was good, yes, but Mohammad was better! Mohammad was the final prophet, who had brought us the last revelation—the only book from Allah that had been dictated word for word by an angel. The Koran was miraculous in its delivery, in its poetry, and in its message. I believed that the Bible had been corrupted from its original content; its erroneous teaching was addressed by the Koran.

So, why do I need Jesus to help me when I believe in the last and greatest prophet of all? I could not shake the question when I went to sleep at night and it was the first thing that came to my mind in the morning.

It began to affect my study of the Koran. And then I began to wonder who told me to call on the name of Jesus.

I needed to deliberately forget this experience and not pursue it any further. I remembered the teaching I received as a child: there are certain questions about Allah that should not be asked, because those questions could cause you to either go insane or to deny God's existence altogether. So I tried to forget it all, but to no avail. I was like an insomniac trying not to hear the clock tick. The more I tried to drown it out, the louder it became:

"Tick, tock. Why did Jesus help you?
Tick, tock. Why did Jesus help you?
Tick tock . . ."

One day, I decided to fast and pray until God answered my question. Every moment I was able to pray, I did. I sat in my cell during the times we were allowed to go out into the prison yard. I restricted myself to one small meal per day, which was not hard because all of the prison meals were small. In the pursuit of this answer, I gave my all to God. The process was mentally and physically exhausting.

"Please tell me, God. Why have you sent Jesus to help me? If I am following you in the wrong way, please tell me what I should do instead, and I will do it. You know I will do anything you tell me. If you just give me the word, I will do it. God, please tell me, God! Am I missing something? Have I followed you the wrong way? God, please don't keep quiet from me. I need to know. I cannot go on in this prison and this life if I am unsure of how I should follow you. You can see how I am trying with all my strength to understand you."

Silence. For two weeks, I heard nothing. There was no guidance, no word, and no direction from God as to what he wanted from me, who he was, or which way was his way. My frustration mounted, and eventually my impassioned pleading turned to anger. When I sought to be visited by the Jinn, they had always come immediately, but with God there was such a protracted silence.

On the fourteenth day of my fast, just past 10:00 AM, I was alone in my cell while the others were in the prison yard. I had reached the end of myself, and in my anger I started yelling and screaming at God.

"You know, you don't even exist! All my life I have done everything to please you. All my life I have done everything in my power to obey you. If you are God, then you should be able to judge the heart! What does it matter really what name we call you or what way we follow? If you can see a man's heart, and you can see that he loves you, then it shouldn't matter! Different faiths are just different routes up the same mountain that we climb to get to you. What does it matter if I climb up one side and someone else climbs up another side? We all get to the same peak.

"But if it *does* matter which way we climb this mountain, and you want me to climb this mountain in a special way, show me and I will do it! I will do it, God. Just show me! But I have asked with all of my strength, and you don't show me the answer. You came two weeks ago and you confused me with the name of Jesus, and I just don't know what to do with it!

"You know what? I have been deceived. You don't even exist! From now on, I am going to do my own thing, like Bobby has."

When we were growing up, Bobby drank, partied, and went around with girls. But not me. I used to look down when a woman passed me on the street so I would not see her face or eyes and fall into sin. If I had a piece of bread I wanted to share, I would cut it in half and deliberately make one of the halves smaller and give the bigger one away.

"You can see, God, how I have done everything I could to please you, but it has never been enough for you. I volunteered to die for you in the Basij! I wanted to walk across the mine field and give my life for you. I wanted to show you how much I loved you by dying for you."

By the time I left Iran at age of fifteen, I had already participated in the hanging of six individuals who had been accused of crimes against the state. Recalling this, I continued my tirade.

"But not only would I die for you, I also killed for you! I had no problem doing anything you asked of me—whether it was to lay down my own life or to take the life of someone else. I would do anything. You know that I would! All my prayers, all my readings, all my study, all my dedication: were they not enough for you, God? What more could I do? What more?

"That's it. I will do whatever I want now. I am going to party, hang around with girls, and have some fun. And when I die, if there is a God, and if there is a Day of Judgement, then you cannot judge me, because it was *you* who confused me, and it was *you* who refused to give me clarity. It was *you* who refused to speak to me and show me the way! How can I be judged, since this is what you have done to me? You are the one who has been silent. How can I follow you?"

"Besides, if you *do* judge me for what *you* have done to me then you would not be just, and if you are not just then what does it matter if I listen to you or not because you will judge me unjustly all the same. I cannot win no matter what I do! I might as well follow my own way."

I thought my case was airtight. Even God could not rebut me.

At the moment of my exhaustion and emotional collapse, when I had no more energy inside of me to do things on my own, it was then that the presence of the Almighty God entered the room. With every fibre of my being I knew I was standing before the one true God. As his presence surrounded me, above all, I felt his holiness. I knew that he was a good God, a righteous God, and a just God. I knew all of my accusations against him were false and that it was impossible for him to judge *anyone* unjustly.

Simultaneously, I realized I was filthy, unholy, and undeserving. I knew I deserved to die. No one passed any judgement on me; it was I who passed judgement on myself. When I stood in God's presence, immediately I knew in my heart, *He is God. He is just and holy! I should die. He should just destroy me. I am the one at fault. I need to be killed. I am the problem here. He should just wipe me off the face of the earth!*

Even though I deserved death, I did not want to die, so I scrambled to the corner of the room and curled myself into a ball, putting my back to the wall. I buried my face in my knees, covered my head with my hands, and cried out, "Forgive me, forgive me, forgive me, forgive me!"

But I knew from my knowledge of Islam that I had committed an unforgivable sin. There was no hope. I was guilty of *shirk*: I had denied the existence of God, declared myself his equal by saying I was going to follow my own way, and I had questioned the holy Koran and the prophet Mohammad. I had questioned everything about God! There was no way for me to be forgiven. I was now an infidel, and I was going to hell. In the same moment, I recalled that in the Koran, even the prophet Mohammad did not have a face-to-face conversation with Allah. The Koran was very clear—Allah does not speak directly to men but only from behind the veil of inspiration or the message of an angel.[10]

This is why the Koran is dictated to Mohammad not from Allah himself, but by the angel Gabriel. I believed that Allah would appear to men for the annihilation of the infidels, so I concluded that Allah himself had come to wipe me off the face of the earth for daring to question him. I kept repeating, "Forgive me, forgive me, forgive me, forgive me!" but I knew there was no hope. Everything I had been taught showed me that for committing the sin of *shirk*, I would now be condemned eternally to the fires of hell. I knew that Allah could not forgive me.

As I continued to plead for mercy, in a state of peril and desperation, at the bottom of the darkest spiral of hopelessness, I felt the touch of a hand on my left shoulder. In common Farsi, a man gently spoke these words to me: "I forgive you." The moment he said these words, it was as if someone had reached into my soul and pulled out all of my guilt, all of my sin, all of my shame, all of my despair. It was all gone. I felt so light! I literally, *physically,* felt forgiven!

"Wait a minute. How can this be? How can this be?"

In Islam, we often use the expression, "In the name of Allah who is merciful and gracious," but we have no certainty of forgiveness in this life. We have to die before we find out if we will be forgiven. The Koran is clear that there can be no assurance for the forgiveness of sin. Not until the Day of Judgement, when our sins are weighed against our good deeds, could we know that we are forgiven. If our good deeds outweighed our sins, then we *might* enter heaven if Allah willed it to be so. In our belief, not even the prophet Mohammad was certain of his fate before Allah.

I looked up into the face of the man who had so lovingly touched me and asked him the question I was asking myself: "Who are you who says, 'I forgive you,' and I *feel* forgiven . . . *today*?"

"Rah, rasti va zendegi," he said in my own language, meaning, "I am the way, the truth, and the life."

This phrase resonated deep within my heart. These words were so profound, so beautiful, and so full of power, but I did not understand what they meant. I had never heard this before.

"I do not understand what that means," I said. "What is your name?"

"Jesus Christ."

With the very mention of his name, I collapsed in a heap at his feet. As I lay there, I suddenly understood all the richness, profundity, beauty, and nuance of his name. It was as if each wonderful word he spoke exploded with meaning in my mind and heart. The two words "Jesus Christ" reverberated within me, and as clear as day I could hear the phrase "the Living God" echoing in my mind. When God speaks to you, every related idea he intends for you to understand is revealed at the instant the word is spoken. With this I finally understood: Jesus Christ *is* the Living God!

I lay at his feet and wept. I had no strength. I wept and wept and wept. I felt a mixture of emotions. On the one hand, I was full of joy and thankfulness for the assurance I had been forgiven of all of the sins I had ever committed. But at the same time, I was angry because I had devoted so much of my life to the passion-filled pursuit of a lie! I had been deceived. Allah is not God at all! With each cry of remorse, wave after wave of peace washed over me. I felt like I had arrived home after a long journey from a far-off country. This was where I belonged. But at the same time I was sad I had been gone for so long and had spent so much time away from the presence of God. I was inundated with all of these emotions. My heart was filled with thankfulness yet ached with remorse and disappointment for all the time I had wasted.

All this time, Jesus stood patiently in front of me, his love and forgiveness washing over me again and again. After what seemed like about two hours, Jesus spoke again.

"Afshin, look up."

I looked up. Suspended in the air was something like a gigantic flat screen television, but without any thickness. On the screen was a moving image depicting people of all nations, generations, and ages. They were from all walks of life and all language groups. The peculiar thing about this image was that as I looked at the people, even though I had never met them, I could see their sins as easily as I could see what they were wearing. It was as if I was temporarily given the ability to see every dark thing that was hidden from other men.

I was completely overwhelmed by this and I cried out to Jesus with a gasp, "Oh, I live among all these sinners!" All I could see was the filth. I was focused on my disgust and feelings of revulsion for these people, but I was still thinking from my old perspective. I thought that there was nothing that could be done: these people seemed so completely beyond hope. They could not be forgiven.

Jesus wanted to teach me something different. He wanted me to know that, although he could see the same terrible things that I could, he was looking past all the sin and was looking at the person. He was looking at his creation into which he had breathed life—the apple of his eye. He wanted to redeem them, and he wanted me to understand his love and compassion for them. So he spoke again.

"Afshin, how easily did I forgive you?"

"Very easily. As easy as drinking water!" I said, using a common Farsi expression. I paused for a moment and then I corrected myself. "No, no, no, no, no! Even easier than drinking water!"

"As easily as I have forgiven you, I can forgive them. Who is going to tell them?"

"I will, Lord!"

"Good. Go, tell them, and I will be with you!"

I got up and ran out of the room, full of excitement. I was so elated and so on fire about this new commission I had been given that I forgot that Jesus Christ, the Living God himself, was standing there talking to me. I didn't stay long enough to see if he had anything else to say, and I didn't even say good-bye. But saying good-bye would have made no sense at all. From that moment onward, Jesus would be with me wherever I went.

CHAPTER 5

Miracles

I ran to the only spiritual place I knew to proclaim the good news about my experience with Jesus Christ—to the prison mosque. I was greeted by my friends there.

"Afshin, welcome! We have been waiting for you. What are you going to teach us today, my brother? Will you be teaching us from the Koran or from the Hadith?"

"Forget Islam! Forget the Koran, forget Allah, and forget Mohammad! I just saw Jesus Christ. He came to me in my prison cell and he told me, 'I am the way, the truth, and the life,' and he can forgive you as easily as he has forgiven me!"

Because I was the leader of the mosque, I thought I would have so much credibility and clout that the other Muslims would immediately listen to me and become Christians also. After all, I had been the most devoted Muslim among them. Surely, since the change was so radical, they would believe me when I said that Jesus had come to forgive me.

Furthermore, the message I was bringing was so wonderful! Forgiveness of all sin, freely, immediately, and with total surety—what a beautiful thing. But they didn't react the way I expected. First, they were shocked, then disgusted, and within seconds the situation nearly turned violent. Everyone was yelling and shaking their fists. They physically ejected me from the mosque and I was not allowed to enter again.

Perhaps things would go better with Mehran, the only Christian I knew.

"Mehran, I have become a Christian!"

"Sure, Afshin, sure you have. What do you want from me this time?"

"No, Mehran, I am serious."

"Yeah, sure, Afshin. Has Khomeini become Christian too?"

"I am serious, Mehran. Really, I have become a Christian."

"Uh-huh."

"Why don't you understand?" I grabbed him with both fists by the shirt and I shook him, pleading with him to believe me. "Really! I have become a Christian, Mehran! Don't you understand what I mean?"

He grabbed me by the wrists and yanked my hands off his shirt.

"So, good for you!" he said.

"Tell me, how do you pray?"

"Why do you want to know? Have you *really* become a Christian?"

"Yes, I saw Jesus Christ."

"Well then, why don't you ask *him*?"

What a great idea. Back at the cell when I had some time, I prayed. "So, Jesus, how do I pray? Do I just take all of my Muslim prayers and substitute your name in place of Mohammad?"

"No."

"Then how do I pray, Lord?"

"Do what you are doing right now. You will understand later."

As time went by I understood that speaking to God from your heart *is* prayer, and is in fact the most *effective* way to pray. I would later learn that Jesus specifically instructs us in the Bible *not* to pray repetitively and by rote.

For the next two weeks, if a question popped into my mind about how I should follow Him, I would simply ask, and I would hear an audible voice answer the question. It was not a voice that others could hear, but I perceived it as audible.

Since I could not enter the mosque, I started hanging around outside of it at prayer times telling the other prisoners about Jesus as they entered and left. I recounted numerous stories about the things Jesus had said, and the miracles that he had done. There was a slight problem though, these stories seemed to be coming out of my head. They just appeared there and I would tell them to whoever would listen.

"Guys, please listen. There was this one time when ten men with an incurable skin disease came to Jesus. They asked Jesus to make them better and he did. He healed their skin disease, right on the spot. And then another time there was a man who was dead, totally dead. Jesus raised a man who was totally dead back to life. It was incredible!"

Story after story, day after day, I would go to the yard and talk to whomever I could. I wondered where the stories were coming from and at one point I questioned whether they were authentic, so I prayed, "Lord, I have no idea where these stories are coming from. I just don't know. They come to me and I say them. I say them for your glory, Lord. Does it really matter if they are true? As long as people believe in you and you are glorified, it doesn't really matter if the stories are true, does it?"

"I am the God of *all truth.* I need no lies to be glorified."

"Oh, I am sorry, Lord. I don't know where they come from. I just say them because they come to my mind. Send me a Bible and I will read it, and I will tell only the stories I read in the Bible."

I prayed this prayer in the evening. At 10:00 AM the next morning, when we went into the prison yard, a man of Indian descent walked up to me. In Pudu prison the non-violent and violent offenders were separated from each other, even during free time. Violent prisoners had their free time on the other side of a large, secure fence. I had never seen this man before. He was not from our section of the prison. This meant that he was a violent offender who had managed to get over the fence.

What does this guy want? Whatever it is, it's bad.

He looked me up and down with a peculiar look on his face. It was as if he was sizing me up for a fight. I put my fists up as if to defend myself and said aggressively in Hindi, "What do you want?" My defensiveness and anger seemed to take him aback. He closed his eyes and cocked his head to the side. He looked a little confused.

"What's the matter with you?" I said.

He reached behind his back, pulled out a book, and said, "This is for you. This is what you asked for."

It was hardbound and had a plain maroon cover with no writing on it. I knew it was a Bible. I grabbed it and ran back to my cell, forgetting even to thank him. I never had the chance, either, because I never saw him again. I was so excited to have that book. I grabbed it, kissed it, put it against my forehead, and clutched it to my chest. Then again, two more times, I kissed it, put it on my forehead, and hugged it. I was overwhelmed with thanks to God for answering my prayer. Sometimes I jokingly say that Federal Express must have gotten the idea for overnight delivery right from God, the author of all great ideas. It was such a beautiful experience for me to learn how quickly and powerfully the Lord answers prayers.

I opened my new Bible, my most precious possession, and realized it was written in a language that was foreign to me. So I prayed, "Lord, thank you for this Bible, but I don't know this language. That's okay. I really appreciate your answer to prayer, but can you send me a Farsi Bible? Then I can start reading it tomorrow when it arrives."

"No, read this one."

"But I can't, Lord. This is not my language."

"Read."

"No, I can't."

"Read."

I was so afraid. The Lord had asked me three times to read, and I had refused. So I decided I would politely show him that I could not read it, and then he would understand what I was trying to tell him. I opened the Bible somewhere in the middle and started reading—and understanding everything I read. This was the first passage I read from my Bible:

> In the year that King Uzziah died, I saw the Lord seated on a throne, high and exalted, and the train of his robe filled the temple. Above him were seraphs, each with six wings: With two wings they covered their faces, with two they covered their feet, and with two they were flying. And they were calling to one another:
>
> "Holy, holy, holy is the LORD Almighty;
> the whole earth is full of his glory."

> At the sound of their voices the doorposts and thresholds shook and the temple was filled with smoke. "Woe to me!" I cried. "I am ruined! For I am a man of unclean lips, and I live among a people of unclean lips, and my eyes have seen the King, the LORD Almighty." Then one of the seraphs flew to me with a live coal in his hand, which he had taken with tongs from the altar. With it he touched my mouth and said, "See, this has touched your lips; your guilt is taken away and your sin atoned for." Then I heard the voice of the Lord saying, "Whom shall I send? And who will go for us?" And I said, "Here am I. Send me!"
>
> —Isaiah 6:1–8

I could not believe my eyes. I thought I was going mad. I saw my own story in the Bible. Isaiah sees God face to face, he is overcome by the conviction that he is a sinful man and that he lives among a sinful people. He is forgiven of his sin with ease and then God says, "Who is going to tell everybody else?" Isaiah replies, "I will!"

I went to Mehran, who knew several languages, to ask him what this book *actually* said. Then at least I could find out if I was crazy or not.

"Mehran, look at this page here in the Bible. Read from here to here but don't read out loud."

When Mehran finished the passage, I said, "Does it say something like this? This man sees God in his temple and he is sitting way up high and the end his robe is so long that it is filling the building. And then the man feels really sinful, and an angel comes and touches a piece of burning coal to his mouth and then God forgives him. And then God asks him, 'Who is going to tell other people?' and then the man says, 'I will.'"

Mehran's mouth fell open.

"Afshin! How can you read this? How do you understand English?"

"Is that English? I don't know how I understand it. I just do."

I was so excited about the new language God had given me. "Excellent! I have learned English!" So I grabbed a local English newspaper to test my newfound language skills. It was complete gibberish to me. I had no idea what the newspaper said, but I could read the Bible.

"God, what is this?" I prayed. "Why can I read the English Bible but not the English newspaper?"

"Afshin, you asked me for a Bible, not a newspaper."

I kept reading the Bible. When I got to the four gospels I realized that all the stories about the life of Jesus I had told to the other prisoners were written there in the same detail. For example, about the ten men with the skin disease, I read from Luke:

> Now on his way to Jerusalem, Jesus travelled along the border between Samaria and Galilee. As he was going into a village, ten men who had leprosy met him. They stood at a distance and called out in a loud voice, "Jesus, Master, have pity on us!" When he saw them, he said, "Go, show yourselves to the priests." And as they went, they were cleansed. One of them, when he saw he was healed, came back, praising God in a loud voice. He threw himself at Jesus' feet and thanked him—and he was a Samaritan. Jesus asked, "Were not all ten cleansed? Where are the other nine? Was no one found to return and give praise to God except this foreigner?" Then he said to him, "Rise and go; your faith has made you well."
>
> —Luke 17:11–19

To my astonishment, I also found that Jesus said, "I am the way the truth and the life. No one comes to the Father except through me" (John 14:6). Jesus spoke the same words to me as he did to his disciples 2,000 years ago.

This is why the Bible says, "For the word of God is living and active. Sharper than any double-edged sword, it penetrates even to dividing soul and spirit, joints and marrow; it judges the thoughts and attitudes of the heart" (Heb. 4:12). When the Bible says that the Word of God is "living," it means that it is more than just ink on paper, more than stories about creation, Moses, the kings, the prophets, and the Christ. It does those things very well. But more than this, it has the power to deliver its message in supernatural ways. It cannot be lost. It cannot be destroyed. When a government confiscates Bibles and prevents their distribution, the Word of God will speak through the Holy Spirit and penetrate the hearts of people anywhere in the world. When we do have a copy of the Bible, it will speak into the moments of our lives in a way no other book can. It is powerful to teach and to respond to our needs.

On the first Sunday after I became a Christian, I wanted to join Mehran for the small Christian service that happened on Sundays in the prison. I was refused entry because I was known as a radical Muslim. So I missed that first Sunday service. Eventually, the group relented and I was allowed to attend church the following Sunday. I did not understand a word of what was spoken during the service. I assume that the chaplain was preaching, but it was not in a language I knew. At the end of the service, people went forward to receive prayer from this tall Caucasian man who was laying hands on prisoners and praying for them. So I walked to the front, and when it was my turn I grabbed him by the wrists and put his hands on my head. I waved my hands in the air, motioning him to pray for me. He took his hands gently off my head and said something to me, which I did not understand. I assume from the context that he was asking what my prayer request was. So I just grabbed him by the wrists again and put his hands back on my head and motioned for him to pray. This time he understood that I wanted prayer, and he just started praying.

The next thing I knew, I seemed to have lost control of my mouth! I had no idea what was going on. I suddenly started saying things I did not understand. For the whole service I had not understood what the speaker was saying, and now I did not even understand what *I* was saying. I was a little frightened at this point, so I clapped my hand over my mouth and made my way out. Mehran followed me.

"Hey Afshin," Mehran said. "You were baptized by the Holy Spirit! You were speaking in tongues!"

"What?"

"Yes, you were baptized by the Holy Spirit!"

"Who?"

"You were baptized by the Holy Spirit. You were speaking in tongues!"

"I don't understand. Just tell me one thing, Mehran."

"What?"

"Tell me—is this normal? Is this okay?"

"Yes, it is."

"Good! That's all I wanted to know."

So many miracles took place in the first few weeks after I became a Christian. I was utterly amazed at the transformation of my life through Jesus Christ. Before I met Jesus, all I could think about was the hopeless misery of that prison: the oppressive heat, the horrible food, the insects, the hard concrete floors, the skin infections, the stench of our urine and feces. I remember all of these things vividly, and how they caused me such despair. But the moment I received forgiveness from Jesus, it was as if someone had transported me out of that prison and I had been set free. I was thankful for everything I had. I was even thankful for the congee in the morning. The food tasted so good to me all of a sudden because I had such a thankful heart. Every day was beautiful. I was so happy and thankful for all of it. Mehran and I would sit and pray together and read the Bible for hours, filled with joy. I alluded earlier to the fact that Mehran had not been walking with God when I first met him. However, after he was imprisoned there was an abrupt change in his behaviour and he recommitted himself to Christ. We enjoyed many hours of fellowship in prison together.

Shortly after this, my brother awoke one morning with a great deal of pain in his jaw. "Afshin, my tooth is killing me and it hurts when I press on my cheek." Bobby's cheek was starting to turn red and swell up.

"That's okay. We can go see the doctor and maybe he can give you some medicine for that. I am sure it will be fine."

When it was clear that Bobby was not going to get better without medical intervention, we approached the prison medical staff. The news of my conversion to Christ from Islam had preceded us, and it was quite offensive to the prison physician, who was a Muslim. Even though Bobby himself had not converted to Christianity, Bobby was refused medical care on account of my conversion. His cheek continued to swell and the pain gradually increased as the infection worsened. The physician implied that if Bobby performed his duty as a Muslim and incited the other prisoners to beat and kill me, then he would be treated. We were frustrated by this but God used it for his glory.

Mehran and I prayed for Bobby and asked the Lord what we should do for him. Bobby was sitting across from me, nursing his face. It was really upsetting me to see him suffering. This empathy for Bobby was something new for me. Prior to this, I had held Bobby in contempt for his sinful lifestyle, his lack of discipline, and his indifference toward Islam. It's fair to say I hated him. I had never cared about his welfare, but now, for the first time in my remembrance, I felt compassion for him. It was really strange. I had never felt love for Bobby, but now in a span of a few weeks, God had totally changed my heart. I loved my brother.

Suddenly, I felt a strange compulsion I could not suppress. I do not know why I knew enough to do this, except that the Spirit of God had placed it on my heart—I certainly had no precedent from my own experience. I got up and ran over to Bobby, placing my hand on his cheek. "In the name of Jesus, go! In the name of Jesus, I say!" with my eyes shut. Immediately I scurried back to my side of the room, covering my face with the Bible.

I wondered if I had done something wrong. Was I supposed to use the name of Jesus like that? While I was cowering behind my Bible, I heard a noise from across the room. *Slap! Slap! Slap!* Bobby was smacking himself on the cheek. *Slap! Slap! Slap!* I peeked over the top of the Bible. Bobby was speechless, smacking his face with a look of bewilderment.

I got up to look. Sure enough, the swelling and redness were gone.

"Jesus has healed you!" I said.

Bobby was stunned. But I am not sure who was more shocked, him or me. There was a quiet reverence in the room. We knew this was a God like no other.

People in the prison knew about Bobby's infection. "Hey Bobby!" they said. "Your face is better. What happened? Did they cave in and give you some medicine?"

"No," he said. "My cellmates prayed for me."

Shortly after this, Mehran and I were praying in the cell together when Bobby came over and sat down beside us, saying, "I don't know what it is about Jesus, but I have experienced his power and I want him in my life."

So there on the floor in Pudu prison, my brother also knelt and accepted Jesus Christ as his Saviour just weeks after I had.

CHAPTER 6

Deliverance

Bobby had given his life to Christ because he had seen how God had changed my heart. He knew the old me and he knew I would never leave Islam. Yet the unimaginable had happened right before his eyes. The fact that I would now voluntarily follow Christ must have meant that I had overwhelming evidence to do so. Bobby also had the testimony of his own physical healing, which was indisputable affirmation of the amazing power of Jesus Christ.

Mehran had gone from being a lifeless Christian who was trapped in a number of habitual sins to a vibrant, enthusiastic, and bold soldier for the Lord Jesus. He prayed with us, he fellowshipped with us daily, and he worshipped with us in the prison chapel. Bobby had been a nominal secular Muslim who did not bother following any rules, but, when challenged, would staunchly defend Islam. I, on the other hand, was a radical and fanatical Muslim obsessed with the rules of Islam. The most beautiful thing about this was that the three of us, despite our extremely different educational and religious backgrounds, grew to be more and more like each other each day, as we became more and more like Jesus (Rom. 8:29).

Saeed, on the other hand, did not *personally* receive any miraculous healing, vision, or dream. But Saeed saw the miracle of how our lives had changed. He saw how we were completely transformed by the gospel working in our hearts. He also saw how God continually answered our prayers and how things simply went better for us after we had given our lives to the Lord Jesus Christ. Watching this unfold made Saeed thirst for Christ.

"I want to know what is going on with you," he said. "I don't know how you can be so content in this place. It is so awful here and yet, for some reason, you guys are full of joy. I can't deny it. Something has happened to you. I have been watching you now for three months. This is all really beyond my explanation."

His spiritual blindness was lifted and he was able to see that the gospel was good news for him also. He knew that the power that had awakened our hearts had to be divine. Prior to Bobby's and my conversion, we had been abusive to Saeed. He was our punching bag—figuratively and literally. But afterwards, we were so much kinder to him that he could not deny that Jesus Christ had changed us. One day in our cell, the time came for Saeed to call on the name of Jesus. It was so beautiful to see how his faith blossomed over the course of the following weeks.

Prior to my accepting Christ, I remember seeing Mehran with his eyes closed in the corner of the cell. I had, at that time, assumed he was napping. Through our new friendship, I learned he was trying to pray incognito. He was terrified of me because he had seen the spiritual darkness that controlled me and how it had negatively affected other people. But now Mehran and I prayed aloud together full of joy, asking God for various things.

We would pour out our praise and gratitude on him for the marvellous things he was doing, or simply because he is a great and mighty God. When Bobby joined us, we were three, and our joy was being made complete, as expressed in 1 John 1:4. Finally with Saeed, we were four Christians in the cell, praying, worshipping together, and praising God.

The four of us held hands, sitting on the concrete floor of the cell, as we were engaged in our prayers and worship—totally oblivious to the terrible heat and humidity. All the things that had previously made us so unhappy—the cramped quarters, the terrible food, the stench, and the abusive staff—they were now insignificant in comparison to the joy that we all shared. It was as if we had tasted of the glory that was to come and we could remain joyful in it, as it is written: "I consider that our present sufferings are not worth comparing with the glory that will be revealed in us" (Rom. 8:18).

We shared all of our feelings and excitement with the last man standing, that is, the only one who had not knelt before Jesus.

"Fariborz, look at what is happening! Look at what Jesus has done in us. Look at the miracle that happened to Bobby. Look at how Afshin has changed!"

"No! I am not going along with you guys on this. It is God's fault that I am here in the first place, and since he has done this to me, I am not going to follow him. I am really not interested in anything else you guys have to say."

After a few weeks of this, Bobby spoke up with a spiritual confidence that I had not seen from him. During one of our prayer sessions, he suddenly turned to Fariborz, who was sitting alone and said, "Fariborz, God is telling me to tell you something. He says he has brought you out of so much crap, and has helped you when you asked him for help. Now, he is giving you his good news. If you refuse it, he says he will send you back to the same pile of crap."

Fariborz was quite confident that our smuggler, Seivash, would ultimately be successful in helping us escape from Malaysia, after we had almost made it a few weeks earlier. So he said, "Oh really, Bobby? He says I was in a pile of crap? And he has told you that he is going to send me back to the same pile?"

"Yes," Bobby said.

"I'll tell you what then. Why don't you send a message to God for me. Why don't you tell him to go right ahead and send me back to Iran. I am not going to become a Christian."

We pleaded with him, and we were truly saddened by the attitude of his heart. It was so prideful. That day was a Monday. When prisoners had meetings with the jail officials they would be called out by their prison number during the time in the yard. On Tuesday morning, among a small group of other prisoners, there was a call for #640—that was Fariborz's number. We were so accustomed to all being called together that the rest of us—Bobby (#641), me (#642), Mehran (#643), and Saeed (#644) all sat down together in a row. When the guards counted off the people they had called, they noticed that there were too many of us. Eventually, they figured out that all the Iranian boys had lined up, but only one had been called. The rest of us were sent back, and Fariborz headed to the prison office.

"Where are you taking him?"

"Iranian ambassador."

He was gone for two hours. By the time he was returned, we were all back in the cell. He looked completely shaken.

"What was the meeting about, Fariborz? What's wrong?"

"The Iranian ambassador to Malaysia came to meet with me."

"And?"

He had a look of total dismay on his face. "They are sending me back to Iran. I can't believe it . . . I can't believe it."

We were all shocked. The significance of what had happened could not be denied. This had an incredible effect on all of us, but especially on Saeed. From then on, he had a holy fear of God. There was no doubt in his mind that his repentance had saved him from a similar fate. Likewise, we all knew that if Fariborz had humbled himself, God would have been merciful to him and spared him. The next morning, Fariborz was deported to Iran. Unfortunately, that was our last contact with him. After that, we were four in the cell.

Our enthusiasm for the gospel was causing a lot of disruption in the prison. In many Muslim countries, apostasy from Islam is punishable by death. Even if we had been free citizens of Malaysia, many of the guards would have considered killing us to be completely legitimate. How much more, then, did they see this as justified because we were illegal migrants from another country! Not only was our own conversion offensive, but we also were telling other Muslims about Jesus Christ. This infuriated many guards and prisoners. Their anger toward us eventually reached the tipping point. One day, during our free time, the guards armed about thirty prisoners with batons and other blunt instruments and gave them permission to beat us—presumably to death. It did not take us long to figure out what was happening when we saw the mob approach us.

"Run!" one of us said. "Run!"

All four of us ran down the hall, trying to escape, but Pudu was designed to be one big dead end. It was only a couple of minutes before we were pinned at the end of a small corridor. We turned around to put our backs to the wall as they were catching up and prepared for the inevitable. We knew that there was no way out: they were three wide and ten deep. All the while we were offering up frantic prayers to God. We were completely helpless, which is always a perfect time for a miracle.

As the group was about to descend on us, one of us started walking toward them, prompted to do so by the Holy Spirit. The other three followed, and suddenly the whole mob stopped dead in their tracks. Everything fell silent. It was like the time when Jesus calmed the storm on the Sea of Galilee (Mark 4:35–40). The next thing I remember is that all four of us were filing out and, as we did, the group parted and made way for us. We just walked right through them. It was so beautiful how the Lord protected us. That day, we gained a more practical understanding of David's words:

> He who dwells in the shelter of the Most High
> will rest in the shadow of the Almighty.
> I will say of the LORD, "He is my refuge and my fortress,
> my God, in whom I trust."
> Surely he will save you from the fowler's snare
> and from the deadly pestilence.
> He will cover you with his feathers,
> and under his wings you will find refuge;
> his faithfulness will be your shield and rampart.
>
> —Psalm 91:1–4

About two weeks after this episode, the prison officials tried a different approach to quiet us down. They called the Iranian ambassador and he came to pay us a visit. Bobby and I were called into the office to see him.

"I think it is about time that you two boys were sent back to Iran," he said. "You know I have the power to do this very easily."

"Mr. Ambassador, we don't want to go back to Iran, please. We would like to move to another country, where we can practice our Christianity freely. You see, we have both met Jesus Christ and he has done so many wonderful miracles for us and, better yet, we have been completely forgiven of our sins! Jesus appeared to me and he told me, 'I am the way the truth and the life.' It is so wonderful to follow him. You should give your life to Jesus too and accept him for the forgiveness of sin."

The ambassador turned every shade of red in his anger. "Stop it! I don't want to hear anymore of this! I am going to have to teach you two a lesson."

The meeting was over.

About a week later, Bobby and I were called to the office and told to get our things together immediately. We initially assumed that we were going back to Iran, as the ambassador had threatened, but after a few minutes we reasoned that we were headed somewhere else. We just didn't know where. They took us to the airport, escorted us past all the security checkpoints, and put us on a plane. We *still* had no idea of our destination. Once we were on the plane, they handed us the same two illegal Iranian passports that Seiavash had prepared for us as a thank you to my mother. They also gave us the same airline tickets that Seiavash had bought, even though those tickets had expired. They even gave us back the $600 that we had on us at the time of our arrest. We didn't ask any questions, but took our seats and waited expectantly for the takeoff. After we were safely in the air, I asked around and found out the plane was going to Nepal. It was May 14, 1990.

In the middle of the night, we landed for a quick stopover. We were permitted to go into the luggage collection area to stretch our legs. There was an official-looking man at a wicket, so I went up and made polite conversation.

"Excuse me, what country are we in?"

"You are in Bangladesh."

I had never even heard of that country before I got to Malaysia, but I met some guys in Pudu who were from there.

"Is it a nice place, Bangladesh?"

"Passport." He motioned for me to hand it to him.

"No, no no . . . I am just asking you. Is this a nice place?"

"Passport!" he said. He was getting agitated with me, so I thought I should comply. The last thing I wanted was another run-in with passport and immigration.

I opened my passport to a blank page in the middle in the hope that he would not bother to look at the photo. Then I slid it across his desk. I did not want him to see the photo because Seiavash had done a rush job on the forgery and it looked so terrible. Anyone could have spotted it as a fake. To make matters worse, I was seventeen years old and the passport said I was in my thirties.

He took the passport and without even looking at the photo stamped it and said, "Three months entry. Go see for yourself."

I pointed to Bobby and said, "That's my brother!" without even thinking about it. This was not too smart because the forged passports did not bear the same last name. The officer didn't even balk. He took Bobby's passport and issued him a three-month entry on the spot. In fact, Iranians were required to have a visa to enter Bangladesh, but of course we had no such permission. He just stamped it. We were in Bangladesh, ready for a new adventure that the Lord Jesus had planned!

Only later did we find out from people who were still in Pudu that the prison officials had misunderstood the Iranian ambassador's instructions. They thought he wanted to deport Mehran and Saeed back to Iran and so they let Bobby and I go. When he arrived a few days later to fetch us, he was furious when the guards brought out Mehran and Saeed. "Where are the other two, the Javid brothers?"

"We sent them to Nepal. We thought you wanted to deport these other two."

"No, I wanted the Javid brothers, you idiots! Now we have to go and try to find them in Nepal!" he said. "I did not want these two."

"Oh, so sorry, but there is nothing we can do now. They are long gone!"

In this way, unfortunately, Mehran and Saeed were left behind.

Bobby and I stood there staring at each other in the arrivals area of the Dhaka Airport, completely incredulous. "Did you see what just happened there, Bobby?"

"Yeah . . . wow. Jesus saved our hides again."

"It seems like he wants us for something."

We had no idea what to do next, but we had no doubt God was looking after all the details for us.

A few moments later, a young woman who was on our flight approached us in the airport and said, "Hey, are you guys Iranian?"

"Yes."

"My boyfriend is Iranian!"

"Oh, okay . . ."

"He is coming here to see me!"

"Your boyfriend is living here?"

"Yes," she said.

"What does he do?" I asked.

"He's a student at the university. He is coming to pick me up in a few minutes."

When the boyfriend arrived, we told him our situation, "We don't know where we are. We don't know anything about this city at all, and it is night time. We need to get to a hotel somehow, but we don't know where the safe parts of town are."

"Don't worry, guys," he said. "I can help you with that." He gave us some names of hotels that would be good for us, and in a couple of days he came to visit us. He showed us the different parts of town, where to buy food, toiletries, etc.

"We are Christians, and we need to find a church because we want to have fellowship with other Christians," we told him in one of our first conversations with him.

"Oh, you are Christians?"

"Yes."

"Okay, no problem, I can find you a church."

A few days later he came over to our hotel with an address in hand, and the three of us hopped into a three-wheeled motor taxi and headed over at midday. When we got out of the taxi, we were immediately struck by the beautifully manicured garden that surrounded the enormous building. We walked up the old stone steps, through the foyer, and into the sanctuary. There was something strange about it though. It was filled with statues of Jesus and other people everywhere. I had no idea what the meaning of all of this was, but I heard a now-familiar voice in my head say, "Do not make images of me."

"Is this the place, Afshin?" Bobby said.

"No."

We turned around to leave, and a man in a long, black robe approached us we were walking out of the building. "May I help you, my son?" he said to me.

"No, you may not." I was polite about it, but I knew it wasn't the place for us. We turned around and walked out. Our friend had given us a second address of another church so we went there immediately.

We entered the church property and were greeted by the groundskeeper. He went in to fetch the pastor. As we waited, we prayed. I found it strange that I was not hearing anything in my spirit confirming that we were in the right place. The pastor eventually came and brought us to his office.

"What can I do for you guys?" he asked.

"Well, two things. First, we want you to pray with us because we have not had any Christian fellowship in almost two weeks since we were released from prison in Malaysia. Second, we have not yet been baptized. We know this is really important so we want to do this as soon as possible. In fact, we became Christians in the prison and we requested to be baptized there, but we were refused. The chaplain told us that if he baptized us the whole Christian ministry to the prison would have been shut down by the government because we were formerly Muslims."

"Well, I can pray with you, but I cannot baptize you for the same reason that they did not baptize you in Malaysia. This is a Muslim country, and the risk of violence against this church is too great if I baptize a former Muslim into Christianity."

In many Muslim countries, Christians can practice their faith freely if they were born into Christianity and can freely convert to other religions, including Islam. However, a Muslim who converts to Christianity is at great risk of violent persecution and this makes some Christians afraid to evangelize. The pastor was kind enough to refer us to another church.

"I am going to help you though. I will send you to someone who will baptize you. He has helped other people in your situation."

So he prayed with us and gave us the name of a church and the pastor who would baptize us. The pastor's name was Asa Kain. When we looked at the address of the church, we were shocked to find out that it was on the same street as our hotel. We got back into the taxi and went back to the hotel. We found out that there was a church service that evening, which was a Friday. When we walked in the door of that church, we felt in our hearts that this was our spiritual home. Bobby and I celebrated with everyone that night—singing and praising God. Pastor Asa went up to the front and asked, "Is there a word of testimony?"

I put up my hand immediately, and he motioned me to stand up and speak. I charged right up to the pulpit and grabbed the microphone from his hand. I was so excited to tell everybody all the things God had done in the last six months. I gave my full testimony, and it took about half an hour. Since this was my first time in a normal church, I did not know that Pastor Asa really wanted a brief testimony. I spoke twenty-nine minutes longer than anyone expected. No one was ungracious to me about this, but I have always looked back on my accidental breach of church culture as one of the funniest but most embarrassing moments of my Christian life.

CHAPTER 7

Protection

A few days after I had given my testimony, we were back in the church to make better acquaintance of Pastor Asa and the other staff. That day, we knew immediately that something was amiss. Some of the church members who had been previously very kind to us were now suddenly cold, and we could not figure out what we had done to wear out our welcome.

We had met an Iranian couple in their thirties who had been very friendly and helpful on the previous Friday. Likewise, we were excited to meet them because we did not know there were other Iranians who had come to Christ. We had never even heard of such a thing. She was employed by the school associated with the church. On that day, however, she really gave us the cold shoulder, not even making eye contact. We could not for the life of us figure out what we had done. Why didn't they talk to us if they had a problem with something we said or did? We were just kids. Why were they being so hard on us?

Eventually, we found out that this woman and her husband were telling the church members about us. "You can't trust those guys. They are making that story up. They want something . . . you'll see . . . they are spies sent by the Iranian embassy to infiltrate our church. Their story is too good to be true. And did you see how they tried to fool us into believing they are brothers? Look at Bobby! He's short and stocky, and his eyes are brown. Afshin is tall and skinny and he has *green* eyes, *so green*! There is no way these two are brothers. You guys gotta wake up and smell the coffee here. We have to keep an eye on them. They are going to get us into trouble."

Nothing in my testimony was untrue, and I had given it with all sincerity, in the same manner I give it now. It was to the glory of the risen Christ that I told the members of my new congregation the things Jesus had done in our lives. Bobby and I knew no other Christ than the one who could at any moment intervene miraculously, so our testimonies did not seem fanciful to us. We were just telling the plain facts about God's power as we had experienced it. After all, the same manner of things was clearly recorded in the book of Acts. We assumed that miracles were normal and happen all the time. We had no reason to believe otherwise. Further, if Satan was so willing to do supernatural things for me in my former life, while he hated me, then all the more would the Creator who loved me intervene with miracles.

It seemed particularly strange that she chose to question that we were siblings. If Bobby and I were not brothers, then my mom had been making breakfast for someone else's kid for a long, long time. Fortunately, we had arranged for my father to call us at the church office. The phone was answered by the lady who was spreading rumours about us, and my father managed to inadvertently clear our names.

"Hello?"

"Yes, this is Mohammad Javid calling. I would like to speak to my sons? Are they there?"

"You mean your *sons* or your *son*?"

"My *sons*. I have two of them."

"What are their names?"

"Bobby and Afshin. I thought they were both there. Aren't they both there?"

"Oh yes, of course, okay, yes . . . they are both here . . . hang on."

The rumours faded quickly and both this lady and her husband apologized to us. Through this experience, I learned an important point. Although Jesus forgives us of all our sins immediately when we confess them to him, the process of learning to follow and imitate him in every way is not instantaneous. The couple who had misjudged us was imperfect, just as Bobby and I were imperfect. We were all works in progress. I learned that it requires consistent, long-term discipleship to bring a Christian into conformity with the will and mind of Christ. This fact was not lost on Pastor Asa. He knew I would need regular and systematic discipleship, which he began in his office that same week.

"Afshin, welcome. Come in. I am glad you are here. Are you ready for your first lesson?"

"Yes, very much so."

"Good. Open your Bible to 1 Samuel 15:22."

I did so and read, "But Samuel replied: 'Does the LORD delight in burnt offerings and sacrifices as much as in obeying the voice of the LORD? To obey is better than sacrifice, and to heed is better than the fat of rams.'"

"Afshin," he said, "Obedience is better than sacrifice."

"Okay."

"That's your first lesson. You can go."

"Uh, I am not sure what you mean."

"Afshin, everything in your life that you are going to do for God is a sacrifice. But God is not interested in your sacrifices. He is interested in your obedience. So make sure you obey everything he says."

"Oh, okay."

"Now go. Come back tomorrow."

"Yes, Sir." I meditated on this: obedience is better than sacrifice.

The next day I returned exactly when he said. I was so eager to obey.

"Afshin, what sort of man do you want to be—a man of the Spirit or a man of the Law?"

"What is the difference?"

"Both men see the same things, Afshin. They come into the same church, and they see the same things that need to be done. They see all that is lacking in the body of Christ. Both see what is wrong and what needs to be fixed. The difference is in their response."

"How are they different?"

"The man of the Law opens his mouth and says, 'These are the things that are wrong. These are the things that need to be done. These are the things we should not do. These are the things we should fix.' The man of the Law makes proclamations and makes sure everybody else is aware of the problems."

"And the man of the Spirit?"

"The man of the Spirit sees exactly the same set of problems the man of the Law does, but the difference is that the man of the Spirit quietly goes about doing something about them. That's the difference."

I was thinking about this carefully.

"Now, which one would you like to be, Afshin?"

"Which one would God like me to be, pastor?"

"He likes the man of the Spirit."

"Good. That's what I want to do and what I want to be."

So Pastor Asa began teaching me daily. What I loved about him was that he was not afraid of the commitment of mentoring. He was not reluctant to take ten or fifteen minutes from whatever he was doing and give his full attention to someone. Whenever anyone was with him, it was as if there was no one else in the world who mattered to him at that moment. His way of mentoring people has affected my life in a manner that cannot be expressed. This one man was willing to pour nuggets of gold into my life on a daily basis. I could come to him without appointment at any time of the day, knock on the door, and ask him questions. He would always greet me with affection, and I would never be made to feel I was intruding on him or inconveniencing him. He loved me and he loved to teach me.

Pastor Asa and I soon had a conversation about Bobby's and my plan to get to Canada.

"So, how are you planning to get there?" Pastor Asa said.

"Well, there is an international soccer match in Indonesia in a few weeks. We are going to tell immigration that we want to go watch the match. Since we have a good reason to travel, they will not likely look at our documents very carefully." I showed him the passports. He looked at them skeptically. "Then we can exit Indonesia and travel through another country or two, and hippity-hop our way to Canada. You see, once you have entered a country, very little attention is paid to your documents on your exit. The Indonesians won't notice, and then we can just keep moving on."

Pastor Asa looked a little concerned. "Afshin, let me ask you a question."

"Yes?"

"Afshin, can God do anything that he wants?"

"Yes, of course."

"Absolutely anything?"

"Yes."

"For example, if he needed you to be in Canada right this second, do you think he could pick you up from Bangladesh and plant you down in Vancouver in the same instant? Could he do this?"

"Oh yes. Absolutely."

"So, if he wants to put you there, let him do it. Let him take you to Canada when he wants. It will be much easier to let God do that work for you."

What a brilliant idea. I didn't need to break the law. I didn't need to help God. He would make a way. "Okay. I will stay in Bangladesh until he makes a way for me to go to Canada."

"Good. I am looking forward to it."

We were able to write to Mehran and Saeed in prison. Through our correspondences with them we found out about the debacle with the Iranian ambassador by which we had been accidentally released. That's when we realized that the Iranian government would be looking for us in Nepal. I still get a giggle out of this when I think about it. Mehran found out through one of the other prisoners that there was another man living in Dhaka who had been imprisoned in Pudu at the same time Bobby and I were. We contacted and met up with him and his friend. That afternoon I decided to go out for a rickshaw ride with the two of them to do some sightseeing while Bobby stayed back at the hotel.

We passed by a park just after dark, and one of the Bengali men asked the driver, "Could you cut though the park? It is a shortcut to where we are going." The rickshaw driver obliged, but as soon as we were a fair distance from the road, the two of them dragged me out and pinned me to the ground—one man on my torso, the other on my knees. The driver just sat there stunned, too afraid to intervene.

For nearly a week I had been fasting during the day and eating one small meal in the evening. I was in the habit of fasting so I could devote myself to prayer. I was feeling really weak. Although I did not have much energy in me to struggle, I fought as hard as I could. Our money and passports were in my pocket. To complicate matters for the robbers, I was wearing army-style pants with buttoned side pockets. In order to subdue me, the one on my chest pinned my arms down with his legs and started to choke me. In addition to the driver's lack of involvement, there were other people in the park watching all of this happen. Why were they just watching? I was not getting much air at all, and at some point I noticed that the muscles in my arms and legs were starting to twitch. I had seen this before.

When I was in the Basij, I had participated in six executions of people charged with political or religious crimes. One of the hangings I assisted in was of an Afghani man. I don't even know if he was guilty. At that point in my life, if someone whom I respected said someone was guilty of crimes against Islam, I never questioned it. If there was a good chance they were an infidel, then to my mind they deserved no mercy. As I watched the Afghani man being hung, I noticed his muscles twitched just before he finally died. Seeing the twitching of my own muscles as I was being strangled, I concluded that I too was about to die. I turned my focus from the eyes of the man choking me and looked beyond him into the heavens. "Lord, I guess I am going to see you. If you are going to take me home now, I do not want to die looking at this man. I want to die focused on you."

As I spoke these words to the Lord in my heart, out of the blue, it was as if someone knocked both of the man's hands off my neck in one swift blow. I was able to get a breath but I had no clue what had happened. The man was persistent though. He grabbed me by the throat again and started choking me. A second time, as I was passing out, I turned my attention to the Lord and said, "Father, I guess I am going to see you," and a second time, the same invisible protector kicked that man's hands from my neck. This time, it was more violent. Both of his arms were flung into the air. My attackers finally got the picture that something extraordinary was happening and ran into the darkness. They got away with all of our money and both passports. I rejoiced though. The Lord saved my life, and fulfilled a second promise from Psalm 91:

> If you make the Most High your dwelling—even the LORD, who is my refuge—then no harm will befall you, no disaster will come near your tent. For he will command his angels concerning you to guard you in all your ways.
>
> —Psalm 91:9–11

Now that those illegal passports were gone, the temptation to continue travelling illegally evaporated. In retrospect, I saw that all of these things were God's will.

After the robbery, Bobby and I had no money. By this time my father had moved to Canada to be with my mother, so we called them in Vancouver to tell them we had been robbed. They said they would arrange to send us some money as soon as possible. The next day we went to the bank to see if the transfer had arrived, but it hadn't. We did not know what to do. We did not even have money for food for that day. We were totally stuck again. It would have been possible for us to borrow money from people for a few days, but they had so little and we could not burden them for long.

So, we started to pray, "Lord, we need you again. We know that you have been the one to bring us through all these things so far, and we know that you will look after us for all the things to come. Please make a way for us to be able to eat until the money from Mom and Dad comes."

Finally, we were so hungry, we just went ahead and ordered room service. We figured we could worry about the bill when it arrived. So we ordered the food, it arrived, we ate, and we were satisfied. Normally, at this hotel, they required payment for food on the spot. Likewise, for the room, they expected payment daily. We were not allowed to run up a tab the way you are in the United States or Canada. To our amazement, the bellhop never came with the bill for the room or for the food. Bobby and I looked at each other, shrugged, and thanked God for room and board. When dinner time came, we ordered another meal, and the same thing happened again. They forgot to bill us for anything for about six days.

Daily, we went to the bank to find out what was going on with our money. We confirmed by telephone that my parents had sent the money, but the paper record of the money transfer had been lost in

Bangladesh. This created a lot of confusion. So, yet again, we trudged up to the third floor of the bank, where all the international money transfers were processed. Compared to modern banks in the West, this one was pretty primitive. There were rows and rows of desks with clerks sitting at each of them. There were no dividers separating any office space, and all transactions were processed on little pieces of paper. We approached one of the clerks, and he casually looked into the status of our situation. He returned empty-handed.

"So, you don't have our money?"

"Sir, I am sure that your money will be found, but we have no record of the transfer. We are looking for it, but you will have to be patient with us. I am certain we will be able to sort this out for you."

"But it's been almost a week. We need money to live."

"I am sorry, Sir. At the moment, this is all that I can do for you. Please come back later today or tomorrow and I am sure we will have more news for you."

So Bobby and I started to leave the bank, again, dejected. As we were walking out of the room, a scrap of paper on the floor was caught by a draft and rolled by Bobby's feet. For some reason, he picked it up and read it.

"Afshin, our names are on this!"

"What do you mean our names are on it? Let me see that."

"Look Afshin, see? 'Bobby or Afshin Javid' and an amount of money is written here. This must be the slip of paper he was talking about."

"You think?"

"Let's go find out." We ran back to the counter.

"Is this the piece of paper you needed to complete our money transfer?"

The clerk looked at the piece of paper quite puzzled. "Yes," he said. "This is what we were looking for. Where did you find it?"

"Over there on the floor."

"Oh, so sorry. Someone must have dropped it."

"No problem, but we will be able to get our money now, won't we?"

"Yes, of course, just a moment please."

We returned to the hotel with about $500. As we walked in, we were approached by a hotel staff–person, who looked a little distraught.

"Sir, sir. I am dreadfully sorry, but it appears we have neglected to bill you for your room for the last few days. I am so sorry but we need payment on the spot. This is very inconvenient, I am sure, but do you have the payment handy?"

"Yes." I said, "No problem." I handed him the money.

"Oh yes, it appears also that you have not been billed for any of the food either. Can you pay this now also?"

"Yes, of course." I paid him the rest.

It was amazing how God looked after us every step of the way. He gave us the ability and the means to live honestly by paying what we owed. He supplied all of our needs.

Sometimes we found out afterward about miracles God performed for us. There was a tall British man in our congregation who had heard my testimony. One day he glanced at the maroon, hardbound Bible I had been given in Pudu prison and asked to see it. He looked at it carefully and opened it to the middle to read a few lines.

"You can read this?"

"Yes."

"And you understand it?"

"Yes."

"Afshin, do you realize this is a King James version?"[11]

"No, what is a King James version?"

"This is a four-hundred-year-old translation of the Bible. This is old English."

"You mean there are different types of English?"

"I am an Englishman, and even I have trouble understanding this."

"Well, I am Iranian and I have no problem understanding this."

It was then I realized that God had opened my eyes to his Word in a more miraculous way than I had initially understood.

CHAPTER 8

The Rainstorm

Because I had decided to follow Jesus, and I had committed to being obedient in all things, it was important that I immigrate to Canada in a completely legal way. All my actions needed to honour the Lord, and I would wait upon him for my opportunity to leave Bangladesh.

To initiate this process, I went to the United Nations High Commissioner for Refugee (UNHCR) office in Dhaka, Bangladesh. After we registered with them, they were able to locate an old file that was created for us at the UNHCR office in Karachi and they had it transferred to Dhaka. It took a few weeks for the file to find its way, but eventually it did arrive. By this time we were making the acquaintance of the UNHCR officer in Dhaka. Naturally, the conversation turned to Jesus Christ and our decision to follow him.

"What?" he said. "You have become Christians?"

"Yes, we have," I said.

"What on earth would possess you to do something so stupid? Everyone knows that Mohammad is the last prophet and the best prophet. Why would you want to listen to any other prophet?"

I gave him a brief version of my testimony and concluded, "So, you see, now I know that Jesus Christ is the way, the truth, and the life. He has forgiven me and he can forgive you just as easily."

"That's ridiculous. You have left Islam to become a *kafir*?"

Kafir—this was not the first or last time I would hear that word applied to me. *Kafir* is a common pejorative term to describe anyone who does not accept Islam, particularly Christians and Jews. The English translation is "infidel."

"You must repent of this and turn back to the true religion. This is a terrible thing that you have done."

Culturally speaking, I understood his perspective. We used to feel the same kind of dismay and disgust when we found out that Muslims had converted to other religions. Even if a non-Muslim failed to acknowledge that Islam was the greatest of the religions, we would be offended, and we would let them know it. Indignation and aggression were the normal way for us to respond to perceived or actual attacks on Islam. So we could empathize with his perspective.

Most Muslims have acquired this kneejerk response from their exposure to the religious and cultural mores of the East. In the Middle East and South Asia, there is a pervasive sense of the need to be loyal to one's religious and social community. People do not consider the needs of an individual in the same manner as is done in the West. Even though the revulsion for apostasy from Islam is learned primarily from the religious culture, the concept is firmly rooted in the Koran and Hadith. Interestingly, the reason most non-Arabic speaking Muslims do not glean these convictions from the Koran itself is because they are most often required to read and memorize it in its original language, Arabic. For this reason, particularly if they are uneducated, they may have no idea what they are reading. Therefore, the cultural experience and the oral teaching they receive plays a much larger role than a Westerner might think.

After our conversation with the UNHCR officer, he was committed to making the immigration process difficult for us. When we made an appointment to see him, he would inconvenience us as much as possible. For example, he would make us wait to see him while he was doing nothing, he would take his time with our paperwork, or he would deliberately fail to do things he had promised us. It wasn't limited to petty, passive-aggressive behaviour, either. He would make his anger known to us with various insults and jabs.

The work that Christ had wrought in our hearts by this time was truly amazing. Our old selves would have been angry and vengeful if someone had done this to us. Before, I would have prayed all manner of curses down on him. But our new selves empathized with him, since we had experienced the same indignation ourselves when we were Muslims. As we would leave that building together, Bobby and I would pray for him.

"Lord, won't you bless this man? We pray that you would open his eyes to the truth of your Son, Jesus. Father, let him see the truth of Jesus, that He might know you, Lord. Just bless him, Jesus. Bless his family, his children, his wife, and his relatives. Put your blessing on him and his household, Jesus."

It was true what Paul wrote, "Therefore, if anyone is in Christ, he is a new creation; the old has gone, the new has come!" (2 Cor. 5:17). Jesus said, "The wind blows wherever it pleases. You hear its sound, but you cannot tell where it comes from or where it is going. So it is with everyone born of the Spirit" (John 3:8). By this he meant that those who are born of the Spirit follow the ways of the Spirit, which cannot easily be predicted or comprehended by man, but their *effect* can be easily felt.

The effect of Christ in our lives was clear. We now felt the urge to pray blessings on the UNHCR officer despite his treatment of us. Amazingly, this paradoxically loving response wasn't specifically taught to us by other Christians. The Spirit of God brought it about. We had been radically changed from our former selves. Strangely enough, we did not even really notice that it had happened—it just happened. It was not until many years later that we reflected on the incredible difference between our old response to conflict and our new response. God simply did it. It was his work. My natural penchant to aggression, anger, and unkindness had become an instinctive response to bless. As Paul said, "Bless those who persecute you; bless and do not curse" (Rom. 12:14). By the Spirit of God, following Jesus' command to love our enemies was not hard. In the same manner that Christ had forgiven us, so also we could easily forgive others. He did this in us and he is owed all the glory.

We prayed for this officer for weeks on end, and we would bring him up as a prayer request in church meetings. One day when I was leaving the UNHCR office, I went to see one of my new friends who worked in the United Nations Development Program (UNDP). This man was a very passionate African Christian.

"Afshin, how are you doing, my brother?"

"Excellent," I said. "It would be impossible to do any better." I realize that this may sound a little unrealistically optimistic given my circumstances at that time, but I really did have a lot of joy. God was doing so much in our lives. This had almost become my signature response.

"Really?" my friend replied.

"Yes. Things are great. We just came from the UNHCR office, and we met again with a man we are praying for. He's trying to cause us as many headaches as he can. But that is okay. Things are still great." I explained that the officer was offended about our conversion to Christ.

"Why don't we pray about this now?"

"Sure," I said, "that would be great."

"Father God in heaven, we bring Afshin before you. He is your precious child whom you have chosen from before the foundation of the world. He is your son and he is your servant. Lord, put your hand of protection over your child. We also pray for this officer, Lord. Father, teach this man a lesson that he cannot stretch his hand out against your children. He cannot persecute your children. Lord, protect your children. Defend your children. Be the shield around your children, Lord. Bring them victory. In the mighty name of your Son, Jesus Christ, we pray. Amen."

"Amen," I said timidly. Something was very surprising to me about this prayer. A little perplexed by this I said, "I did not know that we can pray such a prayer. Can we really pray that God would teach him a lesson? Isn't that a little like cursing him?"

"No Afshin, we are not praying a curse on him. We still forgive him and we still bless him. We are simply asking God to defend us. In his greater wisdom, he can choose to do whatever is best. As his children, we have the right to ask for his protection and defence. It is always our job to love and bless people, and it is God's job to decide when it is appropriate to defend us. He can choose the right time in his sovereignty and wisdom."

Could this be true? Could we ask God to defend us against persecution? Was this contradictory to the commands to "love your enemy" and "bless those who curse you"? My African brother seemed convicted in his heart that we were permitted to pray to the Lord in this manner. His prayer was full of passion, his hands were raised to the heavens, and he seemed to have so much confidence. I thought about this all the way home. Perhaps we could ask God to defend us in a way that was just and holy and, at the same time, we could still love and bless our enemies.

The very next day, I returned to the UNHCR office because I needed to retrieve some information about my immigration case. I went to the office and I asked to speak to the officer who had given us so much grief. He was not at his usual desk. Another person served us.

"I am sorry, sir, he does not work here anymore," the clerk said.

"What do you mean?" I asked.

"Oh, he was fired this morning," he said.

The boss just marched up to him that morning and told him to pack up his things and leave. The motivation wasn't clear because, although he harassed *us* all the time, it seemed to the other employees that *generally* he did his work.

We learned from this experience how willing God was to protect us and show his love for us. I learned that God *does* defend his children according to his wisdom and justice and, all the while, we can still love our enemies and bless our persecutors. He would defend us, and he would do it dramatically if he had to. With each experience of his tender care for us, my love and understanding of him deepened.

Bobby and I eventually moved out of the hotel we were staying in and rented a small apartment that had a shower and a kitchenette. We bought a little television set, and a couple of mattresses we laid on the floor at bedtime. During the day, we would prop one of the mattresses against the wall and leave one on the floor to form a makeshift couch. To get ourselves around the city, we bought a second-hand motor cycle—a blue 125 cc Yamaha.

I don't want to overstate things. These were not luxurious conditions we were living in. There was no sink in the room, just a tap coming out of the concrete wall with a drain below on the floor. The "stove" was just a hotplate. The shower piped in lukewarm water. The conditions were primitive by the standards of the West, but we were happy with our apartment and it became our home.

By this time, Bobby had become friends with a number of Iranian university students who were studying in Dhaka, and he was hanging out with them more and more. Meanwhile, I was spending most of my spare time at the church.

One night I came home from church and laid down on my mattress. It was one of those yellow foam mattresses with a rubbery smell to them. So I was surprised when I laid my head down and smelled the scent of perfume. I knew that Bobby had brought a girl back to our room while I was out. I confronted him immediately.

"Bobby, what's going on? You've had a girl here—alone in this little room. What are you doing?"

"What are you talking about? I never had a girl over. You are being paranoid."

"Now you are lying to me. I can smell the perfume on the mattress. You have had someone over here tonight and you know that is wrong. You should not be alone with a girl like that—especially not in our apartment. Don't you want to obey God and stay pure? This is our house. This is supposed to be a holy place. What you have done has dishonoured God, and you have made his house unholy."

"Why does everything have to be so dramatic with you? Just settle down. You are blowing this way out of proportion."

"I can't live in the same place as you if you are going to be having girls over for parties and the like. I am going to have to go live on my own."

"You are becoming as nutty a Christian as you were a Muslim."

"I just want to follow God and you are getting in the way."

"You are being ridiculous."

"No, I have to leave. I'll tell you what. Mostly you just sit around here and do nothing. So, you can keep everything in the apartment—the beds, the hotplate, the pots, cutlery and TV—everything. I will take the motorcycle because I need to go all around the city for church and Bible studies."

I stormed out of the apartment and Bobby followed me. As I was about to get on the motorcycle, Bobby shoved it and it fell on me. Then he jumped on top of me and started hitting me. I pulled myself free and got to my feet. By this time, he had settled down a bit. I dusted myself off.

"So I guess you want everything, Bobby? You can keep the bike too then!" I turned my back on him and walked away with just the clothes on my back. "You know what? He can keep everything for all I care."

As I walked down the street I was praying for Bobby. "Lord, forgive him. Forgive him for having a girl over. Forgive him for hitting me. Just help him to follow you, Lord. I don't understand. He has seen all the miraculous things you have done, but he does not seem to want to obey you sometimes. Just help him, Father. Bless him, Lord. I want the best for him, but I just can't stay with him."

All the while, I knew God was going to give me a better living situation if the one with my brother was not going to work.

Since then, I learned that there was a big problem with how I dealt with Bobby that day. Bobby was involved in some things that were wrong, but my reaction to him was wrong also. My response was coloured by my background as a strict Muslim, and when I became a Christian, some of my religious culture followed me—the key word being "religious." Religiosity—a devotion to rules-based spirituality—had followed me into my Christian walk, and there were times when I failed to show the same grace that Jesus had shown me. By no means do I wish to convey that I should have tolerated sin without addressing it. Not at all! But it would have been better to calmly but firmly confront Bobby and give him a second chance rather than throwing up my hands and abandoning him.

In this situation, I acted more as a "man of the Law" than a "man of the Spirit," and although he would have been justified to do so, God did not call me out for my behaviour. Rather, he showed me the grace I should have shown Bobby. I have since learned that when we are young Christians, God makes allowances for our ignorance and tolerates some childish behaviour. His expectations of us are not for immediate perfection. Paul writes, "Do not conform any longer to the pattern of this world, but be transformed by the renewing of your mind" (Rom. 12:2). God knows that this will not always be an instantaneous and immediate renewal but a steady and systematic working in our hearts and minds. After twenty years of being a Christian, if I now treated someone as harshly as I treated Bobby that day, I know God would not tolerate it, and would bring it to my attention.

Months later I would find out that on the particular occasion I had smelled the perfume on my mattress, Bobby had not invited a girl into his room alone, as I had assumed. He had invited a friend and his girlfriend over to hang out. I had not even taken the time to find out the facts before I flew off the handle. Nevertheless, even though I had been presumptuous, judgemental, and ungracious toward Bobby, God continued to provide for me. I went to the church and told Pastor Asa what had transpired. He made a few phone calls to see if there was a place I could stay.

There was a wonderful woman who was in her mid-fifties attending our church in Dhaka at that time. She was a Finnish dental surgeon named Dr. Elma, who had been working in full-time medical mission work in Bangladesh for many years. Although she had the opportunity to be rich as a dentist back in Finland, she left all of this to run a free clinic for poor Bengalis. The Swedish mission organization that provided for her needs also looked after the supplies to care for the patients who came to her clinic. Her devotion to her work was tireless. Marriage was not something she appeared to have even considered because her time was completely consumed by her efforts for the Bengali people. Not only this, but she had developed an allergy to the tools and gloves she used as a dentist, and so her hands were constantly inflamed and cracked. Her work days were very painful for her, but she loved the Bengali people so much that she just kept on going. Hearing of my need, she opened up a room in her home for me and let me live and eat free of charge.

Around that time I embarked on an unavoidable conversation with my family. I needed to tell them I was a Christian. I decided to tell my mother first because I knew her reaction would be more restrained than my father's.

"Mom, I want to tell you one more thing before you go."

"Yes, Afshin?"

"Mom, the reason I am hanging out at this church so much is that I have become a Christian. I am following Jesus Christ now."

I explained to her all of the things that had happened and told her that she needed to follow Jesus also. There was silence on other end of the phone.

"Mom, is it okay with you that I am a Christian?"

From the other end, I heard an unenthusiastic "Hmm." It was not clear whether that meant yes or no. The call ended abruptly.

It did not take long before my father got me on the line.

"What is this your mother tells me? Tell me yourself. I can't believe it."

"Well, Dad, I have become a Christian."

"What do you mean by that?"

"Just as I said. I have become a Christian."

"Have you gone out of your mind? You have left Islam? You have left the true religion?"

"No, Dad. I have found the truth, or rather, it has found me. I can explain. I had to leave Islam. Jesus Christ appeared to me."

"What about Bobby? Him too? Have you gotten him mixed up in this also?"

"Yes, Dad, Bobby has decided to follow Jesus also."

"I can't believe you would do this to us. Why would you do this?"

"Dad, you don't understand. I have been forgiven of my sins and you can be forgiven just as easily."

"You have gone crazy, Afshin. Don't call on me anymore until you have come back to the truth of Islam. You are no longer my son. I have no obligation to you anymore."

The conversation ended poorly. He told me that I was going to be treated as if I had died. The irony of all of this was that my father was one of the least devout Muslims I knew. He never did daily prayers. He never read the Koran either. Islam was something he supported as a state religion and a political force, but not as a personal faith. Despite the fact that his personal life was basically secular, he demonstrated the same disgust and indignation for my conversion that the

UNHCR officer had. Many Muslims reacted this way. Even if they were ambivalent about Islam in their personal life, they had a sudden renewed passion for Allah when someone converted to Christianity. Although this made no logical sense, it was the cultural norm and so it did not surprise me in the least. It saddened me, however. My father meant so much to me.

In this way, person by person, the Lord allowed me to be stripped of the family I had relied on. Gradually, he taught me to rely on him alone and on my family in Christ. I was reminded of the words of David, "Though my father and mother forsake me, the LORD will receive me" (Ps. 27:10). Shortly thereafter, I wrote my father a letter to this effect:

> Dear Mr. Javid,
>
> Thank you for your recent correspondence telling me I will no longer have the privilege to call you my father. I want to tell you that this is no problem because now I have a Father in heaven who will look after me and he will never leave me or forsake me.
>
> Yours Sincerely,
>
> Afshin Javid

I never sent it to him. I wanted to speak to him in person. At this point, my father was not sending me any more financial support, so I had to rely on God completely. Fortunately, he had provided me a place to stay through Dr. Elma. When she heard all that was going on she told me, "Afshin, You can stay with me for as long as it takes to sort out your immigration plans. Don't worry about it." This was a great relief to me.

Once Bobby and I had fully registered as refugees with the UNHCR, we were eligible to receive an allowance for our living expenses. Bobby was designated as the person to collect the money for both of us. The problem was, he started keeping my portion for himself. After this happened a few times, I requested that the UNHCR separate our two immigration cases so I could receive my living allowance directly.

Weeks before, when I moved out from the apartment with Bobby, I had been fervently praying for him. "Lord, you know how Bobby is having a hard time following you. He does not seem to appreciate the way you have rescued him from his sin. Father, maybe you should take some of the support out from underneath him and let him fall. When he falls, Lord, I know he will turn his eyes to you again. Father, when he does, reach your hand out and lift him up in your compassion so that he can have joy in you again." Bobby's walk with God steadily deteriorated. He had fallen hard into the same sins that he had struggled with as a younger man, but he had not yet turned his eyes back to Christ Jesus. This was a great sorrow for me.

It was now early in 1991. I was eighteen years old. My father told me that I was no longer his son. My brother was not talking to me. I was a refugee in a foreign country with nothing. There were times when I felt so alone. Although my pastor and my church family did their best to love and provide for me, I was still lonely and sad at times.

One day I borrowed a motorcycle from a friend at church and drove out to a park in Dhaka on the banks of the Buriganga River. I had always gravitated to bodies of water as a place to think, pray, and be restored. Multilevel passenger ferries chugged by while vendors in small wooden boats—shaped like wide-bottom canoes—motored or poled by with their fruit, fish, or other wares. I sat there completely dejected.

"I have nobody," I said to myself. "Everyone has abandoned me. Lord, I am so sad. My whole family is gone. I have nothing and I am nowhere. Look after me, Lord."

I got back on the motorcycle, weeping as I rode home. Thick, billowing clouds were accumulating on the horizon, gradually consuming sunbeams as they encroached on the city. The first droplets produced that familiar smell of evaporating water off hot pavement. A downpour followed minutes later. The rain fell in sheets, with drops so big it seemed they could each fill a shot glass. In seconds, the road was like the surface of a lake, pocked by myriads of little water bombs pelting it from above. I did not have any rain gear or a helmet so I could barely see a thing. As I rode along in the deluge, the rain smacked me in the face.

"Great," I said to myself, "in the lowest point that I have had, here comes a storm to add insult to injury. Now God is punishing me with the rain. I guess I haven't been beaten down enough, so he has sent the clouds to deliver a little extra beating." I was feeling pretty sorry for myself, and I was forgetting how much God had looked after all of our needs coming out of Malaysia and into Bangladesh. It is easy to lose sight of God's kindness in a moment of sadness.

Then the Lord spoke to my heart. "No, no, no, Afshin," he said. "No one is punishing you. Stop for a moment and feel that warm rain wash over you, my son. Quiet your heart and let me speak to you. Just listen."

I paused and let those rain droplets pour over and drench every part of me. I heard the voice speak again.

"Afshin, I am washing away the weight of all the pain you have experienced."

At that moment, all of the burdens I was carrying, all of the sorrow, despair, and abandonment I felt, began to dissolve in that warm rain. The dust of this world that was weighing on me so heavily was gradually being rinsed from my soul. I was reminded how Jesus had washed the disciples feet, gently cleansing the foul-smelling grime that had accumulated from a day of travel. So also he was washing off all of the spiritual sweat and dirt that had caked onto me in the last few weeks. There in the street, riding along in the rain, feeling suddenly refreshed, I began to worship and praise him. Even though I did not have any family to support me, God showed me I had someone on my side that no bad experience, no sorrow, no thief, no prison, and no government could take from me. No one could steal Christ from me. I was my beloved's and he was mine (Song of Sol. 6:3). Jesus was a friend who was closer and more loyal to me than any other person could be. "A man of many companions may come to ruin, but there is a friend who sticks closer than a brother" (Prov. 18:24). So, there I was: a teenager, ploughing through giant puddles on a borrowed motorcycle, getting drenched by monsoon rains, praising the heavenly Father who would never leave him or forsake him (Deut. 31:6).

CHAPTER 9

He Provides

Shortly after this experience in the rainstorm, God again showed his faithfulness to me. My father backed off a bit on his pledge to disown me and began sending me some money to supplement what I received from the UNHCR. Because of my falling out with Bobby, Dad wired money to us separately. This enabled me to make ends meet, but it was tight.

By living with Dr. Elma, I also received the blessing of her live-in help who prepared meals, cleaned the house, and did my laundry. Such help is very inexpensive in Dhaka, and by working for the missionaries the locals generally earned *triple* the wage they could earn elsewhere. In addition, it was not always safe for foreigners to do their own shopping and banking because of the risk of being mugged. This was particularly true for Dr. Elma since she was a single woman. So the hiring of local people was a blessing to the Bengalis, to Dr. Elma, and, by God's grace, to me.

If that was not enough, Dr. Elma also had a driver, so when I needed it, I could even get a ride to church. I could not understand the love that God had lavished on me; it was just incredible. I still had my times of sadness, but I could not deny his grace. The message he was sending me through his loving care was clear—if I was obedient, he would supply all my needs. But what amazed me most was that his generosity had extended so far beyond the basics of food and clothing. Subsequent to this, in my own life and in the lives of others, I have seen that the converse is also true; when we withhold our whole heart from God, we may rob ourselves of the blessings he has for us.

In the fall of 1990, I met the head of the Bangladeshi Bible Society, who was Bengali, and his wife, who was Filipina. After I shared my testimony with him, he invited me to travel around Bangladesh with him to tell my story in towns and villages.

Not long after, we travelled to the Sundarbans—a region in the southwest corner of Bangladesh which literally means "beautiful forest" or "beautiful jungle." The area is famous for its massive tidal mangrove forests and the incredible diversity of wildlife, which led to its designation as a UNESCO world heritage site—both the Bangladeshi region and the adjacent territory in India. This is the home of the famous Royal Bengal tiger, the Indian python, the Water monitor (a large swimming lizard) and even the unusual Irrawaddy dolphin, which looks a little bit like a Beluga. The Sundarbans radiates the glory and majesty of its Creator, and it was my great privilege to travel there.

Strange, new cultural experiences awaited me in the Sundarbans, as they had in all of the other countries to which the Lord brought me. Because the Sundarbans is essentially a giant river delta, you cannot travel for long without needing a ferry ride to the next section of the road. On one such ride, I saw a Bangladeshi "ear doctor" in action. A local gentleman quickly set up shop on the ferry deck, pulling out a bunch of primitive-looking, metal implements which looked to me like they might have come from an undertaker's toolbox. A patient sat down and the ear doctor got to work immediately. After a few minutes of furious effort, he was done. Not only had the patient survived but he also looked very satisfied. He paid the ear doctor, and then the next customer stepped right up. I turned to my Bengali friend and asked, "What on earth is that guy doing?"

"Oh, he's cleaning people's ears," he said. "It's really great. You should try it."

"Are you kidding me? It looks like he's trying to remove the guy's brain or something. You people are crazy for letting a quack like that anywhere near you."

"No, no . . . seriously, you won't believe how much better you will feel."

"You're kidding me."

"No," he said, "it really feels nice when they are done."

So I lined up, sat down, and subjected myself to a few minutes of discomfort. As it turned out, my friend was right. Afterwards I could hear everything so clearly. The whole world was so loud. I guess I had a lot of wax in my ears. That's what happens when you are a teenager.

The ferry arrived on the other side of the river and we headed to a restaurant in a small village. I was still a little squeamish about unfamiliar food at that time, so I decided the safest thing to do was to order chicken. First, I knew the species I was eating, and second, since they would slaughter it right in front of me, I could be assured that the meat would not have been sitting out for too long in the heat. So they killed a chicken for us and prepared it in a curry sauce.

While we were eating, the Bengalis that I was with started complaining bitterly about the curry. "This is too spicy! He put way too many chillies in this. What was he thinking?"

"What are you guys talking about?" I said. "I thought Bengalis were supposed to be tough. You guys are acting like a bunch of babies."

"You'll see, Afshin. This curry is too spicy."

A few minutes later, I noticed that the tips of my fingers were starting to burn and turn red. Then my mouth felt like it was swollen and on fire. As the minutes went on, I felt like I could trace the outline of my digestive system where the flaming hot chillies had travelled.

It was not long before the chillies had frightened my bowels into action, and being a bit of a tenderfoot at that time, I was a little surprised by the so-called "toilet." It was constructed with a simple wooden frame made from bamboo poles, each about two inches in diameter, and had walls made from large leaves hanging from the frame on four sides. There was a hole dug underneath and wooden slats kept you elevated while you were using it.

I raced to it with great urgency but when I arrived, I suddenly found new resolve to "hold it in." The toilet had been in use for some time now and the stench was incredible. Not only that, but every imaginable insect had made its home in the dung heap—it was full of flies, beetles, and other creepy crawlies. Even going to the bathroom was part of the adventure in the Sundarbans.

This problem was compounded by the Bengali tradition of feeding the guest two to three times as much food as everyone else. In order to be polite, I would have to have three helpings at every dinner: rice with vegetables, a second course with white meat, and third course with dark meat. Another difficulty was that big meals were served for breakfast, lunch, and dinner—and all meals were treated as if they were dinner. We ate chicken, fish, and beef for breakfast, lunch, and dinner. I was always so full! I should mention that although I was fed a great deal, the people were very poor. They were generous to us from a state of need not from a state of excess. But as much as I appreciated the food, it often played havoc with my bowels, and when it did I pined for Dr. Elma's toilet.

While we were in the Sundarbans, it was our plan to speak in a few of the churches and some of the smaller villages in the vicinity. We travelled to the home village of my friend, the head of the Bangladeshi Bible Society, and met his family. He was a pastor of a Baptist church, as was his father. Both were men full of God's grace. They were kind and patient in the work they did and how they treated both me and other visiting Christians. I loved being with him and his family. Only in hindsight did I understand the grace that God had shown me by bringing these wonderful people into my life. Along with many others I met in Bangladesh, they were incredible role models; their impact on me cannot be underestimated. Paul writes, "Follow my example, as I follow the example of Christ" (1 Cor. 11:1). These were men who followed Christ with all of their hearts. I could confidently imitate them and know I was on the right path.

It was around this time that I was first exposed to yet another completely foreign concept: the denomination. I did not fully appreciate the manner in which the Church of Christ Jesus had been parsed up until I came to North America, but even there in Bangladesh, I met people who identified themselves as much or more by their denominational affiliation than by their faith in Christ. I had no interest whatsoever in investigating what the various denominations believed, because it seemed to be a distraction from the primary work to which Christ had commissioned me. He told me to tell the world that they could be forgiven as easily as I was forgiven. He did not tell me to figure out which denomination followed the teaching of the Bible most effectively. So I stuck to that original mission.

From the beginning, my approach to the Bible was very simple. Obey what it says, as it says it. Understand it in the most plain and straightforward way possible. The benefit of my refusal to identify myself as anything other than a Christian was that I was able to share my testimony and speak to Christians of all denominational backgrounds. This remains the case to this day.

The next day we went prepared for the ministry event we had planned, and we walked to the location of the church. When we arrived, I asked, "Where is the building we are using today?" There was a clearing with eight or ten bamboo poles erected and strung together with smaller pieces of bamboo. There was a roof made of palm fronds or some other big jungle leaf. It looked like something from a wilderness survival course.

The pastor pointed to the makeshift shelter and said, "That is our church."

"Really?"

"Yes."

People started arriving from all over the place and the worship started about 6:00 PM. For music they used the tabla drums and harmonicas. The people sang earnestly and with such sincerity. It was beautiful to listen to. Although I had been in Bangladesh for about six months by this time, I had not learned much of their language so I could not understand the lyrics. But I did understand the music. I knew they were praising God and I knew that it was beautiful. I just sat there, soaking it up. The worship time went on until midnight, interspersed with some teaching and prayer. Their hunger for praise was so exciting to see. They sang passionately, lifted up their hands, and danced with joy. Doctrinally, they were the strictest of Baptists, but when it came to praise and worship, they were unlike any Baptists I have ever met. It was a wonderful evening.

The next day we visited the childhood friends of my Bengali host. One of these visits stands out in particular. The family lived in a very humble one-room house of mud construction. They prepared us tea and we sat on their dirt floor, spending time getting to know one another. The lady of the house went up to her highest shelf and fetched a small jar of cookies which had been purchased when her husband went to the city. They were extremely precious. The children were not allowed to have them, which is why they were up high. She did not hesitate to offer some to me and, in honour of our visit, the children were also permitted to enjoy some of them. I was so honoured by their hospitality because they were treating us with such extravagant kindness and love. They had so little, but in spite of this they gave us the best of all they had. They knew how to love in spite of their extremely difficult circumstances. The tiny village they lived in was Christian, but it was surrounded by Hindu and Muslim villages which tended to ostracize them. The lack of support from the surrounding area meant that the Christian village did not thrive economically. Despite this, they shared all they had with us. They were such happy people—happy about life in general, and so joyful to have us as guests.

As I sat there, I couldn't help but think I had been brought there to share my testimony and do some Bible teaching, but I had no idea if I was going to be able to teach these people anything. It seemed they had more to say to me with their actions than I had to say to them with my words.

Later, I was invited to speak again in the same village, but this time to a Seventh Day Adventist church. I had never heard of the Seventh Day Adventists, but I was happy to share my testimony with them. The congregation was quite small—maybe fifteen or twenty members. After I had given my testimony, the pastor delivered his message. As usual, I was not able to understand a thing, but something inside me told me something was wrong. In my spirit, I knew the pastor was teaching something that was not from the Word of God. Thinking it would be too hard for me to express myself through a translator, I just kept quiet. After I left, because I did not know how to respond, I just decided to forget the whole incident.

Around midnight I crawled into bed, and in the darkness I felt that the Lord was saying to me, "Come out!"

So I got out of my bed and prepared to go out into the night.

"What are you doing?" my friend asked.

"Oh, I am just going to go out for a short walk."

"Why?"

"I just feel that I need to. I think the Lord is telling me to come out for a few minutes with him."

"Be careful, Afshin. Don't go far."

I did not carry a flashlight or lamp with me. I just walked out into the darkness down the trail. This must have seemed ridiculous to the locals, because the Bengal tigers hunt mainly at night—and they are massive. The average male weighs around 500 pounds and some are said to be strong enough to carry off a small cow. I was actually pretty scared to be walking at night, but I had long ago committed to being obedient to God in all things. "Disobedience is not an option," I said to myself. So I continued to walk.

It was pitch black in the jungle. I kept walking and walking. Eventually I arrived at some water and I felt the Lord say, "Sit down."

"You have not allowed me to use you."

"What do you mean, Lord?"

"You have been in this country for six months and you have made absolutely no effort to learn the local language at all."

"Yes, but this is because I am not going to be in Bangladesh for very long. Why should I invest all that energy when I am going to leave for Canada as soon as possible?"

"Yes, it is true that you do not know how long you are going to be here, but for the past six months, you have refused to learn this language."

"But Lord, I am not going to live here. So what difference does it make if I learn the language or not?" I did not get the Lord's point.

The Lord's concern was not so much the Bengali language. It was that I had hardened my heart to even trying to speak to the Bengali people in words they understood. When I said in my heart, "I am not going to learn this language because I am leaving this country," I had made it impossible for God to use me to the full extent he could have, if I would have had a more willing attitude. I started to understand.

"Afshin, today you were not able to understand what was being taught at the Seventh Day Adventist church, and so you were not able to speak to them. If you had learned the Bengali language, today I would have used you to speak the truth of my words to them. But because of your poor attitude, I could not use you properly."

I suddenly felt ashamed about my stubbornness toward God.

"Lord, will you forgive me for this? I am really sorry about the way I have acted toward you. Forgive me for not doing what I was supposed to do. Forgive me for not being flexible enough to be used by you."

"Afshin, I forgive you. You may go back to bed now."

The next morning, I woke up and greeted everyone.

"Good morning."

"Good morning," the others said.

"How are you doing?"

My friend looked at me quizzically.

"Afshin, you are speaking Bengali. When did you learn it?"

"Ki?" I said, which means, "What?"

"You are speaking Bengali. Since when can you speak Bengali?"

The Lord decided to make up for the lost time—not because I deserved any new gift—but because he wanted to bring glory to his name.

This created an incredible buzz in the local community. I am unsure of how eloquent I was in the Bengali language, but I do know that everyone understood what I was trying to say from that morning onward. In the days and months that followed, I was able to speak to the churches in their own language. It created numerous opportunities to share the Lord with the Bengali people and drew many to hear what God had done for Bobby and me. I even had the opportunity to return to the Seventh Day Adventist church where I had felt so uneasy the day before. I shared with them from the Word of God what I believed would edify and encourage them. As it turns out, my chosen topic was freedom from the Law. It was only later in my life that I understood why this was so appropriate.

It was wonderful to be able to be used by God. Nothing else mattered to me. So when God showed me how my stubbornness stood in the way of him using me further, I took notice. The truth of this principle has been affirmed in my life many times since. My current pastor, Dr. Patrick Safarian, always says, "My greatest fear is that I would become so stubborn toward God's will that he would say, 'I cannot use him anymore,' and would have to shelve me. If I become too stubborn, he will remove me from service in his ministry and he will revoke his anointing over my efforts. I never want this to happen." So he always says to me, "Afshin, pray continually that the Lord would keep you from stubbornness. That way his anointing over your ministry will remain. If you abide in him, his anointing will multiply."

CHAPTER 10

Faithful to His Word

Shortly after this we planned a trip to a local Hindu village to tell them about Jesus. There I was going to have an opportunity to share my testimony. As far as we were aware, no one had ever shared the gospel with this village, and no one in the village where I was staying had actually ever travelled there. It was much easier to speak to Hindus about Christ because the government was not nearly as concerned about Hindus converting as they were about Muslims doing so.

That morning the local Bengali Christians approached me.

"Afshin, today we are going to go fishing in the river. Would you like to join us?"

"I have never been fishing. I have no idea what to do."

"That's no problem. We can teach you. It is not all that hard."

"Well, I don't know if I have the patience to sit for hours and hours in the hot sun waiting for a bite."

"Afshin, we don't fish like that at all. We fish with our hands."

"What do you mean?" I asked.

"Well, come along with us and we can show you."

We set off down the path toward the river, which was a ten or fifteen minute walk. There, the locals had created a hand-excavated pond that was connected to the river. It measured a little over ten feet across and maybe five feet deep. The villagers would chum the water with food scraps to lure in fish. After blocking the exit back to the river with a net, they would wade in and make a big racket by splashing and ringing a bell. As the panicking fish swam desperately into the net trying to make their escape, the fisherman would grab them by the tail or a fin and toss them onto the shore.

After a couple of minutes of being in the water, I felt a sharp pain in my right foot. As a reflex, I lifted up my foot up and then put it back down again. Then I felt a second jab, now accompanied by an awful burning sensation.

"Oww! Oww!" I yelled.

"What's going on?" my friend said.

"I don't know. It's like something bit me and now it's burning like crazy!"

Immediately the locals looked concerned. They seemed to know exactly what had happened. One of the men grabbed me under my arms and dragged me up onto the shore. He jumped back into the water, dove under, came back up with a four-to-five foot snake by the tail, and flung it into the main flow of the river. I cannot say what species it was, but I gather it was one of the venomous sea snakes that inhabit that area. It was clear, however, that the whole group recognized this type of snake and they started preparing to take me to the hospital.

"Where is everybody going?" I said.

"Well, we are getting ready to go to the hospital, of course. That was a poisonous snake. You could die. You need medicine, Afshin."

"Okay, sure we can go to the doctor, but who is going to go and preach to that Hindu village tonight?"

"No one. Forget it, Afshin. We can't go. We have to look after you. Your life is in danger."

"You mean no one is going to go?"

"No. We will just call it off for now."

"Wait a minute! We came down to Sunderbans to preach the gospel. We didn't come down here just to encourage the Christians. We need to go to that village."

"Yeah, but Afshin, sometimes unexpected things happen. We have to take you to the hospital. We can go to the Hindu village another time."

A Bible verse came into my mind: "I have given you authority to trample on snakes and scorpions and to overcome all the power of the enemy; nothing will harm you" (Luke 10:19). I felt that the Lord was telling me that if I went to preach to the Hindus that night, he would fulfil the promise of this verse to me. I was not doing this to test him; I was doing this because I was certain he was telling me to do so. Because I was bitten "in the line of duty," he would cover me with his protection. I would have had no such expectation if I had been bitten by a sea snake while snorkeling, for example. But because I felt that the Lord had spoken, I had complete confidence that we should just go on and preach.

"We don't need to go to the hospital. I came here for the Lord and he has delivered me from all kinds of dangers in the past. He is going to do the same thing now."

"But we should not test him, Afshin."

"I did not come here to test him. I came here to serve him." I trusted him in a totally childlike way. "The Bible says that when we are doing the Lord's work, if a snake bites you, the poison will not hurt you. So we don't need to go to the hospital. We can just go on to the village and preach as planned."

"Afshin, you don't understand. That snake is poisonous, super poisonous. You could die if we don't take you to the hospital."

"The Bible says I am going to be protected. If God is not faithful to his Word, today is a perfectly good day for me to find out about it. If he *is* faithful, he will protect me, and if he *isn't* then I will die, but at least I will have avoided wasting my life serving a God who doesn't tell the truth."

My friend had no words.

My foot felt like it was on fire for about half an hour, but then the pain subsided, and I didn't feel much after that. There were two clear bite marks on the fleshy part of my heel, close to my ankle. My foot swelled and turned red, but that was the end of it. I did not develop any other symptoms.

In North America, if I had told my friends that I was not going to seek treatment for a snake bite, they would probably have tackled me, tied my hands behind my back, and driven me to the emergency room. But in Bangladesh, the people had nothing, so when they became Christians they had to rely solely on God for everything. They had seen many miracles and they had great faith. As a result, it did not seem preposterous to them to take the Bible at its word. When I explained my conviction that God would protect me, not one person in our party disagreed. We readied ourselves for the trek to the Hindu village.

I was able to walk without much difficulty, and I don't remember the pain in my foot being a problem that afternoon. We started out for the village along a trail flanked by a river on the right and the open jungle on the left. We did not know how far it was to get there, so with every person we encountered, we had a conversation that went something like this:

"Excuse me. Do you know how far it is to the next village?"

"Sure, of course. You see the farthest tree there in the distance? As soon as you come to that tree, you just hang a left and it's just a little bit up the road after that."

The first time we heard this, we said, "Oh, great. Not much further." That tree at the end of the road would come and go, and then we would start to worry we had missed something.

We would ask someone else and they would say, "You see the farthest tree there in the distance? As soon as you come to that tree, you just turn left when you get there. It won't take you longer than five or ten minutes after that."

That tree also came and went.

After hearing this from a few more people we just pressed on. We finally arrived after dark. We jokingly concluded that "just beyond that last tree" was a cultural expression for "sixteen miles down the road."

We soon walked up to one of the huts and introduced ourselves. My Bengali Christian friends had brought along some cassette tape players that could be recharged with a hand crank. We had the gospel and some Bible teaching recorded in various languages, and we also had some worship music.

A small crowd gathered around us while we played music and sang songs for them. After this, we told them how God himself came to earth in the person of Jesus Christ, lived a perfect life, and then died on the cross for our sins. I had a chance to share my story also. When we had finished sharing, we asked if we could pray for them.

On our way into the village, we had noticed an emaciated man in his forties lying in a bed on a terrace, all wrapped up in blankets. I don't know what was wrong with him, but his abdomen was obviously distended, and he had that hollow, hopeless look you see in the face of someone who has been left to die. He was so ill that he could not even move. We went up to pray for him as a group.

After we had finished praying for him, he got up and was walking around talking with everyone. He even posed for a photograph. Prior to this, the villagers assured us that he had been completely bedridden and had not walked unassisted for some time. The man himself was so amazed by the way he had been strengthened in the name of Jesus that he decided to give his life to Christ that very night. A year later, I was pleased to hear a report that a small church had been planted there, and that someone was visiting once a week to preach and disciple the new Christians. The man who was dying had been baptized shortly after our departure. He was not completely healed of his disease, only strengthened in the last stages of his life. He seemed to understand this and soon requested a Christian funeral. We were told that at the funeral, the gospel was preached and a number of other villagers became Christians.

The day after we returned from the village, I had no further effects from the snake bite. If being saved from the effects of the snake bite was not enough, it seemed that God had done something else for me that day. From about the age of nine, I had suffered from a chronic, deep ache in the bones of my legs. It did not affect my joints, so I was able to run and play (and get into trouble) but there were some days when it was so bad that I had to stay home from school. I remember it being a constant distraction. I had seen my family doctor and specialists about this in Iran, but I had not received any specific diagnosis. Some physicians had told my mother that it was "rheumatism," but I am not sure if they meant this as just a descriptive term or a specific diagnosis. In any case, they did not prescribe any treatment for it and I was told there was nothing that they could do for me. This had followed me all through my teen years. The beautiful thing was that after the snake bite

I never experienced this pain again, praise God! Sometimes things that look bad on the outside turn out to be a gift in disguise.

In all of these dangers the Lord protected me—from the prisoners who had planned to kill us in Pudu, from the robbers who had taken my passport, and now even from a poisonous snake. As Psalm 91 says,

> You will tread upon the lion and the cobra;
> you will trample the great lion and the serpent.
> "Because he loves me," says the Lord, "I will rescue him;
> I will protect him, for he acknowledges my name.
> He will call upon me, and I will answer him;
> I will be with him in trouble,
> I will deliver him and honor him.
> With long life will I satisfy him
> and show him my salvation."
>
> —Psalm 91:13–16

Many Christians believe that the Bible is speaking metaphorically when it says the Lord will protect us miraculously, but I take it literally. He does protect us, and he will protect us in very tangible ways. Certainly, the Apostle Paul understood these words in a very literal way when he too was bitten by a snake:

> Once safely on shore, we found out that the island was called Malta. The islanders showed us unusual kindness. They built a fire and welcomed us all because it was raining and cold. Paul gathered a pile of brushwood and, as he put it on the fire, a viper, driven out by the heat, fastened itself on his hand. When the islanders saw the snake hanging from his hand, they said to each other, "This man must be a murderer; for though he escaped from the sea, Justice has not allowed him to live." But Paul shook the snake off into the fire and suffered no ill effects.
>
> —Acts 28:1–5

These promises are not written just for the heroes of the Bible. They are promises for all of us who trust him completely and do his will.

CHAPTER 11

The Mosque

We spent the next few months back in Dhaka. Pastor Asa continued to teach me with patience and diligence, and by God's grace I was able to spend a great deal of time at the church. I helped out with the services, attended various Bible studies, and assisted with outreach activities. At every opportunity I shared my testimony for the sake of those who had not met the Lord Jesus, and to encourage people who were already Christians.

I was also blessed to partner in ministry work with two young Bengali men, both of whom were in their early twenties. Kajol had come from a Hindu background, and Pintu, like me, had left Islam to follow Jesus. Pintu decided to become a Christian after listening to a gospel radio ministry in Bangladesh, but I do not recall Kajol's story. Both men had left their home villages to live in Dhaka, because the risk of persecution was lower in the city, where there was relative anonymity.

We travelled together to Chittagong and other towns and villages in the south of Bangladesh. Kajol was blessed with a beautiful voice, and everywhere we went he would serve by singing, while Pintu and I would share our testimonies and teach from the Bible.

Pintu had not told his family he had become a Christian, and for some time he had provided them various excuses to avoid returning home for the celebration of Muslim holidays. Over time, his father developed a suspicion that he had become an apostate from Islam and demanded he return to his hometown of Kushtia for the celebration of *Eid al-Adha* in 1991.

Lots of Westerners have heard of the celebration of *Eid al-Fitr,* which is the feast that marks the end of Ramadan, the Muslim month of fasting. Fewer have heard of *Eid al-Adha*, "The Festival of Sacrifice." Traditionally, each family makes the sacrifice of a sheep, goat, cow, or camel. The animal sacrifice commemorates the willingness of Ibrahim (the Arabic pronunciation of Abraham) to offer up his son Ishmael to Allah, and how Allah ultimately provided a ram in lieu of Ishmael.

It is important to note that the Koran's account of Ibrahim and Ishmael is in disagreement with the biblical account which tells a similar story, but clearly states that Abraham offered up Isaac, not Ishmael (for the full story, read Genesis 22).

Pintu knew there was going to be trouble for him during the *Eid* celebration. "Afshin, I think that I am going to have to go home for *Eid.*"

"Why?" I asked

"My dad strongly suspects that I am a Christian. If I don't go home, he said he is going to send relatives to Dhaka to find me and bring me home by force. I have already gone ahead and bought my bus ticket. I have to go. I am sure pretty sure that when I tell them I am a Christian, they are going to kill me."

"What are you going to do?"

"I don't know. I guess I will go and see what happens."

"Okay, there is only one thing to do," I said.

"What's that?"

"We have to pray! Let's call an all-night prayer meeting at my place. We will pray and fast, and we will ask God for protection for you."

Kajol, Pintu, some other Christian friends and I got together and started to pray. Sometime in the early hours of the morning as we were pouring out our hearts to God, He spoke to me in my heart.

"Afshin. You must go with Pintu."

"What?"

"Yes, Afshin. You need to go with him."

I looked up and saw that Pintu was praying with his head to the floor while I was sitting with my arms around my knees. I interrupted the prayer.

"Pintu, I have something to tell you. I have to go home with you. God wants me to go with you."

Pintu glanced at me but did not say anything.

Maybe he did not hear me.

"Pintu," I said, "God wants me to go with you."

He turned his face toward me for a second and said, "Nope, that is not God saying that. You are wrong. Check again."

I was sure it was God speaking to me. I had not been mistaken about this in the past. But I gave Pintu the benefit of the doubt and I returned to my prayers.

"God, I am quite sure you were asking me to go with Pintu. Am I wrong?"

"You must go with Pintu," he said.

"Pintu, I asked again. He is telling me to go with you."

"No, it cannot be God, because if you come with me, everyone is going to find out that we are Christians and then, for sure, they will kill us. This is Bangladesh. This is a Muslim country. It is not like some of those moderate countries out there. They will kill us, Afshin. Kushtia is a holy city with a huge mosque and a school of theology. My father is a Muslim leader—they are very, very strict. They don't mess around. They *will* kill us. God would only tell you that you should come with me if he wanted us both dead, so it could not possibly be God speaking."

"Look, Pintu, if God has planned for us to die then we are going to go there, and they are going to kill us. I am not afraid of death. Everybody is going to die one day or another somehow. Dying is not a problem. Just because you think he might allow us to die does not mean he is not telling me to come with you."

"How can it be God?" he said. "You can't even buy a bus ticket to get there right now because they are all sold out for *Eid*. I got my ticket ages ago. The seats were sold out months in advance. How can God be telling you to go? What are you going to do, walk there?"

If God wanted me to go, he would provide a way. I just knew it.

"Tomorrow I will go to see Pastor Asa and ask him about this, and you go see if you can find a bus ticket for me," I said. "If you can, then God is saying that I should come with you. If not, then I will stay here."

Pintu was so sure I was wrong that he actually put some effort into finding me a ticket. That way, he could rub my nose in it. Meanwhile, I went to the church to talk to Pastor Asa and tell him what I felt during our night of prayer.

"I always wanted to know what kind of characters the disciples of Jesus were," Pastor Asa said. "You know what I mean? I ask myself, 'What was Peter actually like? And Matthew—what would he say and do?' I wanted to know what kind of personality these men had—who they were and what it would be like to spend time with them. Having met you, Afshin, I think I have a little better picture. You are totally nuts. You have no fear of dying. I like that."

"No, of course not," I said. "If you have fear of death, then you cannot really live. Every one of us is going to die anyway. God has already chosen which way we are going to die. So if he is okay with it, then I am okay with it. He can have it any way he wants."

Pastor Asa and I prayed together about the situation, and later on I caught up with Pintu.

"I looked all over the place," Pintu said. "There were no tickets available. So, on a whim, I just checked with the same bus company I bought my own ticket from. I figured that there was no way there would be any seats left, because they are the biggest bus company, and they would sell out first. So I went to the counter and asked, 'Do you have any tickets left before *Eid*? Any day really, it does not matter. I know that seats are hard to find.'

"'Let me have a look,' he said. 'Oh, yes, we do have one seat on an afternoon bus. Do you want it?'

"'Sure, sure, I will take it. I have been wandering around all day trying to find a ticket.' The clerk began filling out the ticket. I asked, 'By the way, what day is it for?'

"'Thursday afternoon.' he said.

"I realized we were leaving on the same day. That's amazing! It made me think that maybe God *was* speaking to you."

"'What time does that bus leave?' I asked.

"When he told me the time, I was totally shocked. I realized that we were leaving at the same time. I paid him and took the ticket. When I got home, I compared your bus number and seat number with mine. Even though I bought my ticket a few months ago, we are on the same bus . . . and you have the seat right beside me."

There was no denying it. God wanted me to travel with Pintu. This was only the first of many confirmations. The second came on the day of our bus trip. The man across the aisle from me was a Muslim cleric. As soon as I sat down, I introduced myself and engaged him in a conversation. I started by talking to him about God and his faith, and what he believed. Gradually, I turned the conversation to the topic of Christ Jesus and what had happened to me in the prison cell. Pintu became more and more agitated as the conversation went on because he knew that people in the other rows might overhear us. He thought they were going to start beating the tar out of us right there on the bus. But it did not turn out this way at all. Unlike many other people with whom I had shared Jesus, this man did not even bristle. In fact, he seemed really interested in what I was telling him. He was clearly ready to hear about Christ, and no one even seemed to be bothered about it.

We arrived at Pintu's home town and proceeded to his parents' house. Pintu knocked timidly on the door. His father opened the door and greeted him. I also stretched out my hand and greeted him with a standard Muslim greeting, "*As-salamu alaykum,*" meaning "Peace be upon you." Pintu's father left his hands at his side.

"Are you a Muslim?" he asked.

Without any hesitation, I replied with a question. "Do you mean 'Muslim by name' or 'true Muslim'?"

He looked perplexed. He had never heard anyone give such a cryptic response to this simple question. "What do you mean?" he asked.

"Well, Muslim means 'submitted to Allah.' Are you asking me if I am a Muslim by name, that is, am I someone whose father read the *adhan* [the call to prayer] in his ear when he was born, and for this reason is called Muslim? Or are you asking me if I am a true Muslim, that is, someone who recognizes the Creator of heaven and earth, who testifies that he alone is the true Creator and has all power? That is, are you asking me if there is only this one God and whether I have submitted myself fully to his will and desires? As far as I am concerned, that's what a true Muslim is."

"Okay, are you a true Muslim?"

"I am a true Muslim."

He reached out his hand to me and said, "*Wa Alaykum as-Salaam,*" meaning, "and upon you be peace." He welcomed us in, walked us through his yard, and into the back where there was a meeting room which doubled as a bedroom at night. There was a carpet on the floor for sitting, and over the doorway hung a curtain so there would be no distraction if the women of the household happened to be in the yard. We sat and talked. Within a few minutes there was a tap on the wooden frame of the doorway. Pintu waited for a few seconds and then retrieved the food and a bucket of water that had been quietly placed at the entrance by one of the ladies.

We washed our hands with the water and then ate and chatted together. As we spoke, I noticed that Pintu's father kept staring at the floor. There was something wrong. He looked so sad.

"What is wrong with your father, Pintu?" I asked Pintu quietly.

"He is sad because two of my nieces are sick."

It is quite common in Bangladesh for children to develop such severe dysentery that the fluid loss cannot be overcome by simply drinking. If a child cannot be hospitalized and given intravenous and appropriate medications, he or she will simply die. Two of Pintu's nieces were having terrible diarrhea, and his father was very worried about them.

"We must do something about this," I said. "We must pray for them." I started to get up to find out where the girls were so that I could pray. Pintu grabbed me by my left wrist and pulled me to the ground.

"Afshin, they will find out. They will kill us right now if you go pray for these girls."

"If we're going to die, we're going to die. Let's do our job. Don't worry about what will happen. If the time has come for us to go, then we will go."

I turned to Pintu's father and said, "Every man and every woman has a different purpose and a plan for their lives, because God has called each of us for different things."

"Yes," he said.

"Jesus had the power over all sicknesses, and we know that he healed all the sick people he met."

"Yes, this is true too."

"He had the power to raise the dead, in fact."

"Yes," he said again.

"He had the power to heal the blind."

"True."

"Today he holds the same authority he did in the beginning. Would you have a problem with us praying over your granddaughters in the name of Jesus?"

Normally such a question would have led to indignant shouting and threats of physical harm, but he could not stand to see the suffering of his grandchildren, and even though our request to pray in the name of Jesus was completely unorthodox, he said, "No, I have no problem. Please pray."

Darkness was settling in when we left the meeting room and walked through the yard to another building where there was a bedroom housing the girls. They were lying side by side on a single bed and, though the room was unlit, we could see they were in terrible shape. The family did not want us to go anywhere near them for fear the illness might spread, so we stood in the doorway. Pintu and I raised our hands in prayer, flanking his father, me on the left and Pintu on the right. We brought the children before the Lord, and when we had finished, the room actually looked brighter. I mean this literally. It was as if the room had been lit by a gentle, warm light.

During the course of our prayer, both children got up, and when we opened our eyes, they were actually standing together on the bed. They were completely restored. The strange thing was that Pintu's father had left the room. Pintu was still there with me, but his father had actually backed up about fifteen paces. He was now in the middle of the yard, and his knees were shaking. He was absolutely terrified by what he had seen. We knew what he was thinking: Who are these people? How can they pray and receive immediate answers?

Pintu and I were overjoyed. After his father composed himself, we returned to the meeting room and sat down again to talk. I was quite relaxed and continued to eat. Pintu looked like he was thinking about what colour of coffin he should pick because he was sure we were going to die momentarily. A few minutes later there was another knock on the doorframe. Pintu muttered, "That's it. I am sure they have come to kill us."

In fact, it was Pintu's sister knocking. She had come to let us know her mother was running from neighbour to neighbour, telling them what had just happened. Apparently there was another person in immediate need of prayer. The widow down the street had a twenty-year-old son who was very ill, and the doctors had abandoned hope for him. Hearing that the two girls had been healed, the widow wanted us to come pray. I don't know what his specific diagnosis was, but the widow's son had blood in his urine and stool and he was also coughing up blood. The doctor told her there was absolutely no chance of survival and so they had quarantined him on the balcony to die.

We walked up into the house to meet the young man's mother. We told her, "We are people just like you are. We are normal human beings. There is nothing different or special about us. We have no power of our own. We pray in the name of Jesus Christ, and in fact, the Bible commands us to pray for the sick. We don't know why he answers some prayers and not others. But he has commanded us to pray, and so we obey. If your son is healed, you must make a commitment to us: that you will give the glory to the One to whom the glory is owed. You must tell everybody that it was Jesus who healed your son—not anyone else. No other person, just Jesus." She made the promise.

We laid hands on her son and prayed. When we were finished, we went home to Pintu's parents' house. The next day was Friday, June 21,1991—two days before *Eid* celebration would take place. We all travelled together to the mosque for Friday prayers. On the bus ride along the way, I knew there was a good chance I would die that day, because God had impressed on me some things to say that would make me very unpopular. I was not too concerned about it. I trusted God to protect me.

When we arrived, I asked if I could take some photos of the inside of the building—just in case I actually did survive the trip. Some of the people in the mosque protested, "This is a holy house and no one has ever taken any photos of it. We cannot permit this."

"Which is holier—this mosque or the *Ka'aba* in Mecca?" I asked.

"The *Ka'aba*, of course. It is the most holy house."

"Yes, the *Ka'aba* is the most holy house of Islam, and you know that there are photos of the *Ka'aba* in books, in mosques, and even in movies all over the world. Do you set your own mosque above the house of Allah in Mecca?"

"No, of course not."

"So, then is it okay to take a few pictures?"

"Well, perhaps it is alright. Go ahead."

I took a few pictures and sat respectfully, waiting for their prayer time to be finished. When it was all over, I stood up among the crowd of about 3,000 men.

"Brothers, the sacrifices that we make on this day commemorate the sacrifice that Abraham first made. God told Abraham to go and offer up his own son on the mountain. He took his son, built an altar, covered it with wood, and laid his boy Isaac on it."

Immediately there were people in the crowd who shouted, "No, it was Ishmael, not Isaac! He offered up Ishmael! Ishmael was the offering!"

"No," I said, "it was Isaac."

"No, Ishmael! It was Ishmael!" they yelled.

"Remember, my brothers, Ishmael was not the miraculous son. He was the son of Hagar, who was a young woman. It is not uncommon for a man to have children by a younger woman. We all know that an old man can bear children from a younger woman without any problem. The miracle was this—that Abraham had a son from his wife, Sarah, when she was a very old woman. Not only that, she had been barren all of her life—all the more reason for her to be unable to conceive a child. If an elderly, barren woman bore a child, then no one could deny it was God who had given Abraham that son. So Isaac was the most important son to Abraham and to God. When God asked for a sacrifice from Abraham, naturally He asked for the *best* child, the child of the miracle."

At that point, half of the people began shouting, "Beat him! Beat him and his friend to death. Let's just kill them right now!"

Some others were saying, "No, no, no! It does not make a difference. Both Ishmael and Isaac were the sons of Abraham. It would not matter which one he offered. Let him continue. Let's see what he is trying to tell us."

We were permitted to continue. "The ultimate and final sacrifice was not Isaac. It was the ram God provided for Abraham. This was a sign for Abraham and for us that, although God requires us to be willing to offer our own lives as a sacrifice to him, it would be *him* who would provide the offering that would atone for our sins. God would be the one to pay. Jesus was that lamb God provided. When Jesus was sacrificed on the cross, *he* became the fulfilment of the picture he had shown Abraham a few thousand years earlier."

With this, even those who had been diplomatic a few minutes earlier yelled, "The others were right! We should have beat them and killed them right away!"

Things turned ugly. They grabbed us and began yelling and screaming at the top of their lungs, "Beat, them! Kill them! Infidels!" as they surrounded us.

Pintu turned his back to mine. "What are we going to do?"

"The only thing we can, Pintu." I looked up to heaven and quoted Jesus in the same manner Stephen had, because I was sure I was about to go the way of Stephen. "Lord, forgive them. They do not know what they are doing."

As I looked up, the Lord gave me a vision. I saw his face and he said to me, "It is not time yet."

I thought to myself, "He must not see what is happening here."

"No Lord," I said, "I am going to come home because in the next few minutes, I am going to be dead."

Jesus repeated his answer, "It is not time yet."

Immediately I remembered what was written about Paul. "They stoned Paul and dragged him outside the city, thinking he was dead. But after the disciples had gathered around him, he got up and went back into the city" (Acts 14:19–20). With this in mind I thought to myself, "Uh-oh, this is going to hurt," but I was convinced that God would spare our lives.

At that very moment, a large group of women, who were waiting outside, rushed into the mosque. The men parted the way in astonishment. This was a big breach of protocol. Women were not allowed in this mosque, and we were later told that none had ever stepped foot in there. When they rushed in, the men did not want to be defiled and immediately withdrew themselves.

In the front was an old woman shouting, "Don't touch these men! Don't touch them! These are men of God!"

It was the widow whose son we had prayed for the previous day.

"You men know how my husband died. You also know how all the doctors had given up on my son. These men prayed for my son and they said that they have no power of their own. They told me that if my son was healed that I must tell everybody that Jesus had done it, that Jesus had healed him. Well, you can come and see for yourself! Yesterday he was dying on my front porch, but now he is swimming in the river. I am his mother and I can tell you I have never seen him as healthy as I see him today. Jesus has healed my son. Do not touch these men!"

With this, the leaders spoke quietly with one another. After a few minutes, they brought a chair for each of us and told us to sit down outside the mosque.

"We are going to bring some sick people to you. We want you to pray for them to see what happens." They wanted to see the power of Jesus for themselves.

A long line-up of about one hundred and fifty people formed. We prayed for person after person. We could see that most of those who came were sick, but we did not see any immediate, miraculous, on-the-spot recoveries. We do know, however, that there must have been many whose health was restored, because the Muslim clerics were so amazed by the subsequent reports they received that for the next six days they invited us to their homes to speak. They even ordered their families to come and hear teaching about Jesus and the gospel.

CHAPTER 12

Obedience

Pintu was stunned to see all the Lord had done through our act of faith and obedience. Objectively speaking, anyone would have said that our decision to travel to *Eid* was a death sentence. What we did appeared totally irrational, but there was no doubt the Lord's hand had directed us to go. *Eid al-Adha* was a celebration of Abraham's obedience to God. Likewise, God had asked Abraham to do something totally irrational: to offer up the life of Isaac on an altar. Abraham knew this made no sense at all. God promised him that a great nation would come from Isaac. How could this happen if Isaac was dead? Further, we know from the Bible that the Lord detested the practice of human sacrifice that so many of the contemporary pagan religions demanded. God's request seemed totally inconsistent with all he said and would later say. But Abraham obeyed God anyway. It was out of this obedience to anything the Lord said that God was able to foreshadow the sort of sacrifice he intended to make on our behalf. So, when Isaac asks, "Father . . . where is the lamb for the burnt offering?" (Gen. 22:7), Abraham's answer gives us a glimpse of God's plan to save humanity: "God himself will provide the lamb for the burnt offering, my son" (Gen. 22:8). In this we see Abraham's faith in God's mercy for *that* moment, and a prophecy of how he would show his mercy through his own son, Jesus, "the Lamb of God, who takes away the sin of the world" (John 1:29). Abraham's obedience allowed God to work mightily in that moment, and by this means his story has blessed hundreds of generations.

Pintu and I learned that being obedient to God may at times mean doing something that appears completely reckless. In fact, it was in response to our unquestioning obedience that God had worked so greatly in the hearts of the people of that city. Riding back to Dhaka on the bus, we realized when we walked in God's will he would go before us and knock down every barrier—nothing would stand in his way. He had honoured our childlike faith.

Not every Christian is called to do the sorts of things that Pintu and I did. But no Christian should rule out the possibility that God might call him or her to something equal or greater than what I have described here.

I learned that the greatest thing I could ever do for the kingdom of God is not an objective achievement, like building a ministry with a million members, or running a church with ten thousand attendees, or writing a book that starts the next worldwide evangelistic trend. The greatest thing I can do for him is to be obedient—joyfully obedient. He just wants us to do what he says. When we do, the results will be so far in excess of anything we could have dreamed that we will wonder why we ever considered going our own way.

Even Jesus, who is perfect, demonstrated obedience to his Father in heaven. He said, "For I have come down from heaven not to do my will but to do the will of him who sent me" (John 6:38). This was both obedience in life and obedience in his death, as he said, "Father, if you are willing, take this cup from me; yet not my will, but yours be done" (Luke 22:42). In this way, Jesus became a template for us to imitate, as the author of Hebrews says, "the author and perfector of our faith." And as Paul writes,

> Your attitude should be the same as that of Christ Jesus: Who, being in very nature God, did not consider equality with God something to be grasped, but made himself

> nothing, taking the very nature of a servant, being made in human likeness. And being found in appearance as a man, he humbled himself and became obedient to death—even death on a cross!
>
> —Philippians 2:5–8

The greatest protection we had from all manner of danger was to walk in obedience to God. But the most beautiful thing about this whole experience was not the great number of people who heard the gospel, the numbers of people who followed Christ, or the group who had received physical healing. It was not the impossible circumstances of the bus ticket or the miracle of the women running in to save us at the last moment. It was the fact that the Lord God Almighty gave me an opportunity to obey him—and he was pleased with our simple obedience, our childlike faith, and our trust in the *literal* interpretation of his Word.

For me, the greatest of my "achievements" (for want of a better word—none of it was *my* accomplishment at all) in Pintu's home town was that God enabled me to trust him and obey him. This experience completely reoriented how I looked at God and his will. I had a different level of trust for him after this—to a height I would never have imagined on my own. I knew he would always deliver and that I never had to doubt him.

God does not care about *what* we achieve. He cares about *how* we achieve, or rather, how *he* achieves things through us. God did not measure my success in things humans can count, but in what counted to him, namely, my submission to his will. This is why it is possible for a small offering to God to be worth more than a great one:

> As he looked up, Jesus saw the rich putting their gifts into the temple treasury. He also saw a poor widow put in two very small copper coins. "I tell you the truth," he said, "this poor widow has put in more than all the others. All these people gave their gifts out of their wealth; but she out of her poverty put in all she had to live on."
>
> —Luke 21:1–4

God looks at the attitude of the giver, not the size of the gift.

Obedience brought us joy—deeply meaningful and lasting joy—joy from above. I found this joy addictive. I wanted more of it, and I knew how to get it: by obeying more. It was a good addiction. In fact, this joy was a specific promise of the Lord Jesus: "If you obey my commands, you will remain in my love, just as I have obeyed my Father's commands and remain in his love. I have told you this so that my joy may be in you and that your joy may be complete" (John 15:10–11).

I am sure you have noticed how joyful a person acts when he or she first finds love. We love Jesus by showing him our obedience, and when we do so, our romance with him never grows old. We find new joy every morning.

Whenever I tell my story, people always ask, "Did all of those Muslims give their lives to Jesus?" The truth is, I have no idea what happened afterward. To me, the question overlooks the story's most important take-home message, which is that God honours obedience. When I was praying and fasting, the Lord told me, "Go with Pintu." He asked me to do a very specific thing, and I did it. In my own reasoning, I concluded that he was asking us to die, and I had every expectation that this would be the case. Not only did we live, but we had an opportunity to share the gospel with thousands of people and witness a whole bunch of miracles.

If God worked so mightily to allow his Word to be preached to these people, then he is certainly trustworthy to take care of the follow-up and shepherding. I will not be surprised if those people come up to me in heaven and say, "Later on I had a dream about Jesus and I decided to follow him" or "We decided to pray in the name of Jesus, and we saw many miracles, and we gave our lives to him" or "I prayed to Him in the quiet of my house and I was saved." For the Word of God never returns void (Isa. 55:11).

When we returned to the church in Dhaka, we told everybody the story, and they were all so excited about what the Lord had done. We were all so joyful about these things. Shortly after this, I was on my way to church one evening and I had nearly run out of money. I had twenty taka, which is worth about thirty cents in the U.S. After bartering, something I could now do with great expertise, it cost about seven taka to get from Dr. Elma's house to church on a tricycle rickshaw. By the time I arrived at church, I had thirteen taka left. This was an evening service, and when it came time to put money in the offering, I asked, "Okay, Lord, how much do you want me to give?"

"All of it," he answered.

"Sure, I will put in six taka and then I will have seven for the trip home."

"No, I asked for all of it, Afshin."

"Okay, I guess I need to walk all the way home then. No problem, Lord. I can do that." The walk home was about three hours, and it was dark. I was a little nervous about this, but I wanted to be obedient. I put the thirteen taka into the offering bag, leaned forward, and prayed. My elbows were resting on my knees, my eyes were closed, and I had my hands folded against my forehead. I was just spending time talking with him while the offering was finishing up—thanking him for his goodness and mercies to me. Just at that moment, I felt my shirt move a bit, but I did not make anything of it. When I opened my eyes, I looked in my pocket and there were fifty taka there. I had no idea where it came from. I don't know what happened. Maybe someone slipped it in while I was praying, but there was no one sitting around me. I guess it does not matter, really—whether through a person or a miracle, God had multiplied the extra seven taka back to me by seven and one-seventh fold.

So in this instance, again, obedience became the key to the success of the Christian walk, and there has never been a moment in my walk with Christ that I have ever regretted obeying God. But I can unequivocally say that every time I disobeyed God, I regretted it. I have had many regrets. I desire and pray that for the remainder of my life I will obey him.

CHAPTER 13

Abbas

Bangladesh was a wonderful place to be stuck. It was a proving ground for me in so many ways. The Lord taught me over and over that when we are willing, he will work, and mightily so. When I look back on it now, I realize that Bangladesh was the best thing that God could have done for me. Initially, I wanted nothing more than to continue my illegal migration through Asia and on to Canada to be reunited with family. According to what I have been told, my immigration should have happened more quickly than it did. Initially, I was a minor, only seventeen years old. My parents were landed immigrants in Canada, and I was registered appropriately with the U.N. as a refugee. At the beginning, I was told it would be a three-to-six-month process to get me to Canada.

As I spent more and more time in Bangladesh, and as I met so many Christians who were sold out for the Lord, I realized the incredible value of being there. I was so thankful to be part of such a powerful community of saints that it did not bother me much that my family was nearly 7,000 miles away and that Bobby and I were having differences. God showed me by his Word, his Spirit, and the example of all of the other Christians that we needed to be salt and light to the people of Bangladesh.

I met an Iraqi gentleman named Abbas, who was ethnically Kurdish. Because of government-sanctioned persecution of Kurds, Abbas had been deported from Iraq to Iran because he had Iranian heritage.

He had a very strong Arabic accent and spoke only broken Farsi, but this is how we communicated. As Abbas and I became friends, we would hang out together, along with his friend Hassan, another Iraqi Arab. Not long into our relationship, my friends and I began to share the gospel with Abbas and Hassan. At first they were not interested to hear anything about Jesus. Abbas' heart had been terribly hardened by the experiences of the Iran-Iraq war and the persecution he had faced as a Kurd. In fact, he had personally committed numerous atrocities against both the Iraqis and the Iranians.

"I hated the Iraqis, Afshin. They were the ones who had caused my people so much suffering and had killed so many of them. I wanted to have revenge on them, so I enlisted in the Iranian army after I was deported. At nighttime I would go on foot to the front lines and slit the throats of Iraqis, removing their ear as evidence of the kill.

"But at the same time, I hated the Iranians, because they too had oppressed the Kurds. When it was convenient, I would just switch sides and go kill Iranians, cut their ears off, and bring them back to the Iraqis."

When Abbas had his chance, he escaped from Iran to India, where he earned his living selling drugs. Abbas was very interesting because, despite the fact that he was essentially a mercenary, at times he demonstrated unusual compassion for others.

There were a lot of displaced Iranians living in India, Pakistan, and Turkey at that time. They all had the same aspiration—to raise enough money to pay for a human smuggler who would take them to Europe or North America. Oftentimes their hopes were dashed by people who would pretend to be smugglers, take their money, and then disappear, leaving them penniless. To worsen matters, there had been a huge flood of people leaving Iran because of the Islamic revolution. Many Iranians fled to other countries. Families would be stuck for years as displaced persons with no money, and very little hope of obtaining legitimate refugee status with the United Nations because of the sheer numbers of them. To generate income in this desperate situation, many of the women would turn to prostitution simply to help their families get by. This, of course, brought the added burden of shame and dishonour to the women and their families. Displaced Iranians faced hardship at every corner.

Despite all expectations to the contrary, Abbas could not stand to watch them suffer. He would often take money that he had earned from selling drugs and give it to poor Iranian families for food, clothing, and shelter, and most importantly, to escape from India to the West. He was a very interesting character. On the one hand, at times he showed no loyalty to anyone but himself. On the other hand, he would have flashes of incredible compassion and generosity—a Robin Hood of sorts.

Abbas also made money by providing information to various embassies. For example, he would go to the Iranian embassy, introduce himself as a former Iraqi soldier, and sell them information. Likewise, he would go to the Iraqi embassy, say he was an Iranian Arab, and sell them information. If that were not enough, he would go to the Saudi embassy and give them information about both Iran and Iraq. At the peak of his impertinence, he tried to do the same at the American embassy. Eventually, he ended up with enemies on all sides, and they all wanted to give him a proper beating. He had to flee India entirely. This is how he had ended up in Bangladesh, where I met him.

I knew that deep in his heart, Abbas wanted to be good, because I saw the compassion he had for those who were suffering. Shortly after our introduction, I shared my life story with him, and although he found it interesting, he did not fully understand the implications for himself. He did not see that the forgiveness of Jesus Christ was for everyone—that all men had to come to God by means of Jesus.

My church friends would often invite him over for dinner to hang out with them. We did this frequently. At the end of one of these evenings, Abbas, his friend, and I went back to Abbas' place, a room in a small hotel in the lower part of Dhaka. As the night was drawing to a close, we spent some time praying together for Abbas' friend, who had a specific need. At the end of my prayer, I wanted to spend a little more time before God, and so I quietly prayed in tongues. When everyone had finished praying, Abbas looked amazed.

"That was my mother tongue! You were praising Jesus in my mother tongue! How do you know it? Where did you learn my dialect?"

"What?" I said.

"I did not know that you speak my mother tongue! Why didn't you tell me?"

"I don't know what you are talking about."

"When you were praying, Afshin! You were speaking my language! You were praising Jesus in my language. I understood everything you were saying!"

"Ohhh," I said, "Now I understand. You mean when I was praying at the end, there?"

"Yes!"

"Abbas, I was praying in tongues. Sometimes God allows us to speak other languages during prayer as a testimony for those who can understand it. Sometimes, when I pray that way by myself, I don't know exactly what I am saying, but I know in my spirit that I am worshipping God. Sometimes, like now, the words are for someone else—someone like you. I don't speak your mother tongue."

But God certainly spoke Abbas' mother tongue, and this was the turning point for him. He gave his life to Jesus that night. It was wonderful to see how God so beautifully and personally spoke to him. Our group of Farsi and Arab-speaking Christians who had left Islam grew and grew. As one would come, miracles would follow and serve as a testimony to others. When new people would come to the church, everyone was so welcoming. The kindness that Christians demonstrated to newcomers was one of the most beautiful things about Bangladesh. They experienced the love of Christ and then they lavished that same love on others. They did as Jesus taught his disciples: "Freely you have received, freely give" (Matt. 10:8). Likewise, they acted as one body, in fulfilment of Christ's prayer for the church:

> My prayer is not for them alone. I pray also for those who will believe in me through their message, that all of them may be one, Father, just as you are in me and I am in you. May they also be in us so that the world may believe that

> you have sent me. I have given them the glory that you gave me, that they may be one as we are one: I in them and you in me. May they be brought to complete unity to let the world know that you sent me and have loved them even as you have loved me.
>
> —John 17:20–23

The church was not simply a place of Sunday gathering. It was not a club where we would have a 90-minute social gathering once a week. It was where we as a family sat and ate together—eating spiritual food. Nearly everyone at the church was a foreigner who had left his or her country, lifestyle, and the comforts of home all for the sake of Jesus.

The allegiance to Christ I witnessed there was on a different level than I have generally observed in the developed world. People in Bangladesh did not withhold their time, activities, money, and energy from Christ Jesus, but gladly laid it down for the sake of the gospel. As their dedication to Christ increased, so also did their love for people. Jesus said, "Do not store up for yourselves treasures on earth, where moth and rust destroy, and where thieves break in and steal. But store up for yourselves treasures in heaven, where moth and rust do not destroy, and where thieves do not break in and steal. For where your treasure is, there your heart will be also" (Matt. 6:19–21).

As the treasure of the church became Christ, their hearts were drawn to people, because people are the treasure of God's heart. You cannot be dedicated to Jesus without having love for people. As John writes, "We love because he first loved us. If anyone says, 'I love God,' yet hates his brother, he is a liar. For anyone who does not love his brother, whom he has seen, cannot love God, whom he has not seen. And he has given us this command: Whoever loves God must also love his brother" (1 John 4:19–21).

For someone like me, who had never been to any other church in any other place, this sort of dedication, love, and kindness seemed completely normal. This was the standard by which I measured all other churches. Any outside observer would say the people in that church were completely dedicated to the work of Christ. Of course, no one is ever one hundred percent dedicated, and no one has achieved perfection, but I can say with all confidence that it would have been difficult for non-Christians to observe the behaviour of my church family in Dhaka and find fault. They gave all they had to Christ, and when the Spirit of God would bring to their attention something more, they would obey without the same kind of struggle and turmoil you see in the Western Christian. They were the city on a hill, and their light caused many to glorify the Lord. As Jesus said:

> You are the light of the world. A city on a hill cannot be hidden. Neither do people light a lamp and put it under a bowl. Instead they put it on its stand, and it gives light to everyone in the house. In the same way, let your light shine before men, that they may see your good deeds and praise your Father in heaven.
>
> —Matthew 5:14–16

I assumed that all churches in all countries would function in exactly the same way. The church in Dhaka affected me so deeply, without their even realizing it. I have looked back and drawn from this well of wisdom over and over in the years since I left Bangladesh.

An excellent example of this was an American husband and wife who administrated the church school. They could have lived very well in the United States, but they chose the poverty of Dhaka so they could have the opportunity to teach poor Bengali children. Another American couple was from a military background, who had abandoned secure employment and a guaranteed pension to serve the Lord. They left everything to work as Bible teachers in Dhaka. They would preach the gospel, take in strangers, and disciple new believers. Although the American missionaries had very little in common with the Bengali people by way of upbringing, common interests, taste in food, and sense of humour—all the things that usually facilitate relationships—they loved them in the most selfless and wonderful way.

In so many ways, my church in Dhaka reminded me of the early church described in the book of Acts. But what did the early church do so right? Why were those Christians so effective? It is not that they had a different gospel; the message of the gospel has not changed. It is totally unchangeable. I am a sinner, I stand condemned before a holy God, Christ died for me, and if I repent and follow him, I will be forgiven, and I will have life (a spiritually abundant life) both on earth and in heaven. In fact, if we try to alter this gospel, it will become completely powerless and we will be totally adrift. If we tie it to prosperity, to a particular spiritual gift, to specific traditions and practices, or to works, then we make the gospel powerless and therefore no gospel at all. If we make it about anything other than what Christ came for—that is, he came to forgive our sins so he could give us his abundant life, his joy, and his peace—then we will just be inventing a new religion.

What makes a church powerful, effective and right before the eyes of the Lord is the level of love in the midst of the body. Love created the oneness and unity that Christ had prayed for (John 17:20–23)—both in the early church and in my church in Bangladesh. Indeed, Jesus had specifically said love would be the distinction, the hallmark, and the proof of authenticity for his followers: "A new command I give you: Love one another. As I have loved you, so you must love one another. By this all men will know that you are my disciples, if you love one another" (John 13:34–35). Just as governments use special paper, holograms, watermarks, and fluorescent ink as proof that their banknotes are legitimate, so also love—both for Christians and for the lost—becomes the proof of authenticity that the church is functioning in obedience to God. You can see this love in the unity and generosity described in the book of Acts:

> All the believers were one in heart and mind. No one claimed that any of his possessions was his own, but they shared everything they had. With great power the apostles continued to testify to the resurrection of the Lord Jesus, and much grace was upon them all. There were no needy persons among them. For from time to time those who owned lands or houses sold them, brought the money from the sales and put it at the apostles' feet, and it was distributed to anyone as he had need.
>
> —Acts 4:32–35

The Bengali church embarked on the journey of becoming less about self and more about God. Just think about the picture that the term "self-centred" creates. Self-centred people desperately desire to be the centre of attention, but the irony is that others are usually so turned off by them that they leave. In the end, the self-centred person always ends up alone. But the term "God-centred" evokes a totally different image. When God comes, he always comes with an entourage. In all places in the Bible where the throne of heaven is described, whether in Ezekiel 1, Daniel 7, Isaiah 6, or Revelation 5 or 14, God is at the centre of worship for all living things. The throne of God is the focus of the twenty-four elders, living creatures, the angels, the thousands upon thousands, the ten thousands upon ten thousands (Rev. 5), and the 144,000 (Rev. 14). With self at the centre, man is totally alone, but with God at the centre, man is always in a rich community of love.

CHAPTER 14

The Blind Shall See

During one of our Friday evening services, a young blind Bengali man in his late twenties or early thirties tapped his way through the entrance of the church with a cane. He sat and listened to the service, and at the end he came forward during the prayer time. One of our members greeted him at the front.

"How can we pray for you?"

"I was born blind, but I would like to see. Can you pray for me to be able to see?"

"Of course we can pray for this," someone said.

"Yes," I said, "there is no reason why you cannot be healed today. There are plenty of stories in the Bible where Jesus healed incurable diseases, including blindness. There is no reason why he can't do it today."

There happened to be a doctor in attendance who was visiting our church. Having overheard the story, he felt he needed to protect us from embarrassing ourselves and making God look bad in the process.

"Everyone should know that if this man was born blind, it probably means he had an infection in the womb that destroyed his retina, or maybe he has some other inherited problem. Whatever the cause, the nerves from his eyes cannot carry any signal to his brain. The connections are broken. I don't think that praying is going to work here."

"I really don't understand what you are trying to explain to us, and further, I don't want your thoughts to stand in the way of us trying to pray for healing," I said.

"It's like the plug for a lamp," he said. "If you cut the cord, you can't get any power to the lamp. Praying for this man is going to put us all in an awkward position. When nothing happens, we will have to explain why. It would be better to not pray at all."

I didn't understand anything about how eyes work, how nerves work, or how the brain works—and I still don't. What he was saying was all mumbo jumbo. I only knew one thing, James 5:14–15 says, "Is any one of you sick? He should call the elders of the church to pray over him and anoint him with oil in the name of the Lord. And the prayer offered in faith will make the sick person well; the Lord will raise him up."

It does not say, "Pray only for people with certain diseases." It says, "Pray for the sick." For me, praying for the sick was as simple as that: "Pray for the sick." It did not seem all that complicated. It was not my responsibility to be certain that God was going to do what I asked. It was my responsibility to be obedient to his command, which was to pray.

Sometimes God does not heal but says, "My grace is sufficient for you, for my power is made perfect in weakness" (2 Cor. 12:9), and other times He says, "Yes, I will heal." Why he says what he says, and how he answers prayers are his business. These are management decisions. I am a soldier. I don't get to make management decisions. I just have to do what I am told.

So I turned and said, "Doctor, I don't care what you say. I am not deterred by the specifics of this man's medical problems. I am approaching the One who created this man, and I am asking him for healing. I can assure you I have no power of my own to do anything. I just take orders." I felt a little bad for the doctor. I understand that as a medical professional and an intellectual, he was trying to protect us from making fools of ourselves. He was trying to help us out. But sometimes, too much knowledge has a negative effect on our ability to take God at his word.

We all gathered around the man and prayed a very simple prayer: short, to the point, in faith, and in obedience. "Lord, would you stretch out your hand and heal this man in the name of your Son, Jesus Christ. Please give him back his eyesight, Lord."

The next thing we knew the man said, "I can see something! It's kind of blurry, but I can see!"

We all immediately burst into praise and shouts to the Lord. We were so excited to see such a miracle happen right in front of us.

"Hallelujah!" people were shouting.

"Praise God!" echoed around the room. It sounded like the home team had won a football game.

The doctor tried to calm us all down and assure us that we were completely deluded.

"Hey, everyone, just settle down. There is no way this man can see anything," he assured us. "Look, I will show you." The doctor raised four fingers in front of the man's face. "How many fingers am I holding up, sir?" he said. Without waiting for a response, he looked over to us smugly. He was certain that the man would not be able to answer.

"Four," the man said.

"You see? He can't see anything." The doctor looked down at his own hand and realized he was holding up four fingers. I must confess that the fact that the doctor could not remember how many fingers he had held up added to the moment in a most gratifying way.

I am not sure who was more shocked—the man who had been healed or the doctor. Jesus performed this miracle for the Father's glory in the same manner as when he was living among us: "As he went along, he saw a man blind from birth. His disciples asked him, 'Rabbi, who sinned, this man or his parents, that he was born blind?' 'Neither this man nor his parents sinned,' said Jesus, 'but this happened so that the work of God might be displayed in his life'" (John 9:1–3).

Sometimes, as Christians, we try too hard to protect the reputation of the God we serve. Because we are afraid he might not answer our prayers, we avoid praying altogether. We don't want anyone to say, "Your god does not exist," or "Your god never answers." That day I learned we should never assume the role of God's protector and defender because it may lead us to misguided inaction, preventing him from doing a miracle. On the flip side, many have tried to defend God with misguided action, and in so doing have wrongly shed blood in his name. It's best to let God defend his own reputation, and do only what he commands.

This experience built my faith tremendously. After that day, I fully believed that whenever I had the opportunity to pray for the lame, the blind, or the sick of any sort, they would be healed instantly and restored to health. I thought of these words from Scripture: "And these signs will accompany those who believe: In my name they will drive out demons; they will speak in new tongues; they will pick up snakes with their hands; and when they drink deadly poison, it will not hurt them at all; they will place their hands on sick people, and they will get well" (Mark 16:17–18).

I assumed that healings such as this one would be a normal occurrence for the rest of my life. After all, there was no indication in this passage that these would occur only some of the time.

Not long after, I was invited to a friend's house and met another blind man. Immediately, I thought of the wonderful healing that had occurred weeks before. I said to myself, "God is going to perform another miracle."

I greeted the man with enthusiasm and told him the story about the man whose sight had been restored. As I began to share, I hoped that the story would build enough faith in his heart that he would ask us to pray for him in the name of Jesus. Since he was a Muslim, it would be highly unusual for him to allow us to pray for him in Jesus' name.

He happened to be highly educated, which was unusual for the Bangladeshi people, and he also was blind from birth. In the middle of the testimony he interjected, "I see."

I leapt to my feet and shouted for joy, "Hallelujah! Thank you, Jesus!"

He reached out and grabbed my hand. "No, no, no! I see!" he said.

"Yes, praise God! Hallelujah!"

"No, I said, 'I see.'"

"Yes, praise the Lord, you see!"

"No, I see. I see."

"Yes, I know, you see."

"I mean, 'I understand you.'"

I could not figure out why he kept repeating himself over and over, but with this, I pieced the obvious together. I had learned English from my Bible and from the Bangladeshi people, but evidently I did not have all the idioms down pat. From then on, it was indelibly etched in my consciousness that the expression, "I see," could be used to mean, "I understand." After regaining my composure and settling down, I did pray for him, and to my surprise, he was not healed. On the way home, I was really puzzled that the Lord had not answered my prayer, and I was embarrassed for jumping the gun. But I learned another important lesson. God does not answer every prayer. He answers those he sees fit to answer. It is not my job to question him, but simply to pray for the sick as he had commanded, and to thank him for whatever he sees fit to do.

Perhaps the miracle did not occur because the man I was praying for was well-off and educated. I cannot say for sure, but I am often asked why so many miracles occur in Bangladesh and not in Canada and the United States. Bangladesh is an extremely poor country, and unlike the West, medical care is not widely available. Obviously, the need for the average Bangladeshi to depend on the Lord to supply his or her practical needs is far greater. Out of this need, they spend more of their time relying on him in prayer. Because of this reliance, their relationship with him is naturally close. In the West, we don't have the same manner of need. Why should it surprise us that we see fewer miracles?

Naturally, everyone is encouraged by hearing stories of the lame walking, the blind seeing, and the dead rising. Of course, we want these things to happen in our own lives. Not surprisingly, we are drawn, and sometimes driven, by a desire to see miracles. In some circles, we even measure the success of a person's ministry, church, or organization by the number of miracles we can attribute to it. Sometimes we want miracles so badly we imagine ones that are not even there.

In this sense we have moved our focus from the Father who gives the gifts, to the gifts themselves. Rather than praising, glorifying, and exalting him, some of us spend our energy seeking miracles. Make no mistake—because of his love and care, he wants to heal our pain and suffering. Because of his great compassion, he moves in the realm of miracles and wonders, and demonstrates himself to be the God of the impossible. But this does not mean that signs, wonders, and miracles are things we should specifically pursue. In fact, when people approached Jesus and requested frivolous miracles that served no particular purpose beyond dispelling doubt, he rebuked them, sometimes harshly:

> Then some of the Pharisees and teachers of the law said to him, "Teacher, we want to see a miraculous sign from you." He answered, "A wicked and adulterous generation asks for a miraculous sign!"
>
> —Matthew 12:38–39

Other times he did so more gently:

> Philip said, "Lord, show us the Father and that will be enough for us." Jesus answered: "Don't you know me, Philip, even after I have been among you such a long time? Anyone who has seen me has seen the Father. How can you say, 'Show us the Father'? Don't you believe that I am in the Father, and that the Father is in me?"
>
> —John 14:8–10

So, miracles are never something that should be pursued for their own sake. What should we pursue above all, then? We can see it embedded in the Lord's prayer.

> This, then, is how you should pray: "Our Father in heaven, hallowed be your name, your kingdom come, your will be done on earth as it is in heaven. Give us today our daily bread. Forgive us our debts, as we also have forgiven our debtors. And lead us not into temptation, but deliver us from the evil one, for yours is the kingdom and the power and the glory forever. Amen."
>
> —Matthew 6:9–13

After addressing God as "Father," (an intimacy with God that is totally unthinkable to a Muslim) our job is to make the name of the Lord hallowed—that is praised, venerated, glorified, and revered. This is our first task in prayer; not to make requests, not to ask for his intervention, but to praise his holy name. Our second task is to ask him to bring about his will on this earth in the same manner that his will reigns in heaven. Practically speaking, in my life this is achieved by submitting my own will to God's. Only after praising God and submitting ourselves do we present our requests for provision, care, and protection—of which miracles may be a small part. So there is no suggestion in The Lord's Prayer, which is our template for prayer, that we should be making miracles a priority. We should be praising God and obeying Him above all. Signs and wonders will be a natural by-product of following Jesus, because wherever the Lord walked, miracles followed him. So, if we walk with him, we will see miracles.

I learned these lessons from my discipleship with Pastor Asa Kain and other members of his congregation. They sought to glorify the Father, beginning with their own heart, soul, mind, and strength—everything they had. With the same singular purpose, they sought to honour God in their families, then their church, their neighbourhood, their city, and their world.

I shall never regret the time I spent in Bangladesh as a refugee, because I learned so many valuable lessons. The lessons were not without cost. It was hard being separated from my family. It was hard not having any money sometimes, and not having a secure plan for tomorrow. It was difficult living with ambiguity. And, as I have described, I had some really scary run-ins with people who wanted to kill me. But having experienced all of these rotten things, I never look back with bitterness or anger toward God. I only remember how God allowed me to have peace and joy in the midst of these troubles and trials—these difficulties common to all men. I remember all the beautiful lessons I learned and I remember how he delivered me so many times by his own hand. This is our God. No more do I have to run to him and say, "God, I have a big problem." Rather, I can say, "Problem, I have a big God! He will deliver me. He will hear my cry and rescue me."

Chapter 15

Restoration

One day one of my non–Christian Iranian friends asked me, "Afshin, I am looking to buy some American money so I can travel back home. Do you have any I can buy from you?"

At that time, the banks in Bangladesh would not sell American currency to residents unless they could display proof they were leaving the country immediately, and in these circumstances they offered a poor exchange rate. So I suggested, "Why don't you just buy it from the money changers or something?"

"There is so much counterfeit money around. I don't want to risk buying it from anyone I cannot totally trust."

"Well, a lot of the foreign missionaries I know have American money. They often need to buy taka. Do you want me to see if I can get some for you?"

"Sure, that would be great. At least then I would know it was real."

I went to one of my American friends and described the situation. Since he had plans of exchanging his money at a bank, he agreed. Bangladesh had a great deal of crime at that time.

Expatriates leaving banks just after a withdrawal were a common target. Thieves would watch for people who looked Western, wait for them to leave the bank, and then rob them. It was said that the bank tellers were often involved in the process: when a large withdrawal was made, they would tip off their friends with a description of the target individual. In exchange, they would receive a cut of the money. So the idea of being able to exchange money in his living room sounded great to my friend.

I returned to my Iranian friend, told him how much the missionary was willing to sell, and my friend gave me the correct amount of taka according to what he considered a fair exchange.

When I went back to the American, I gave him the taka. When he had finished counting it, he said, "Afshin, this is way too much. I just called the bank and they were offering me 10% less than this!"

"Well, this is what my friend thought your U.S. money would be worth, so all the better! You can have more."

"No, Afshin, that's okay. You did the work. You keep that for yourself."

I did not feel good about this, so I returned to my Iranian friend and told him that the American felt he had been overpaid, and I offered to return the extra taka.

"No Afshin, really it is okay. Anywhere I would have bought it, it would have cost me the same. The fact that I know that I have real American dollars is good enough for me. Don't worry about it—you can keep it."

I could not believe it. In a matter of under an hour, by brokering a currency exchange, I had made 10% on the transaction, which in this case was 150 U.S. dollars. In the early 1990s in Bangladesh, this was a huge amount of money. So I began to offer currency exchange to expatriates and missionaries as a service that would take place in the safety of their homes. I could offer people better rates than the bank would and I could still come away with a decent profit. Everyone was happy.

This ended up being a very successful business. Financially speaking, I went from just squeaking by to a point where I actually had an abundance: all the money I needed, and more. In this way, I was able to help the Bangladeshi people, as well as the church. God provided this blessing not so I could keep more, but so that I could give more. At times I felt that I couldn't give the money away fast enough before the Lord would fill up my pockets again.

While things were going well for me, in my heart I was still unhappy because I knew Bobby was not doing well. When I was a Muslim, I did not respect the way he lived, and so I avoided even talking with him. But now I loved him. It grieved me deeply that our relationship was fractured, and that he was struggling with the same old sins that had always dogged him. I could not rest knowing he was suffering spiritually. Even though I was walking with the Lord, this was not enough for me. I wanted to be reunited with Bobby, and more than this, I wanted Bobby to be reunited with God. My prayers turned toward Bobby even more than before, and I interceded for him daily.

One day he showed up at Dr. Elma's house, knocking on the door. The guard who minded the door came to me, "Afshin, your brother is at the door. Should I let him in?"

He was hesitant, because on his last visit a few months earlier, Bobby had lost his temper at me and broke my television.

I said, "Please let him in. It's okay."

Bobby came in and sat down. We ate together and talked until late in the afternoon. It was so nice to see him after all this time. As it was getting dark, he got up to leave and I said, "Bobby, you don't need to leave. It's my prayer time. Would you like to join me?"

"If I could join you, that would be awesome!"

The Lord had answered my prayers. God's faithfulness had remained. Bobby had struggled, but all the while the Spirit of God had been at work deep within his heart. Bobby and I began praying. After a few minutes, he knelt down on the floor and started to sob.

"What is it, Bobby?"

"I am just tired, tired of all of this. I don't want to do these things anymore. I want to live for God."

I began to weep with him and we continued to pray together. At some point, I leaned over and threw my arms around him. Both of us were weeping as we hugged and we both gave God glory. Bobby knew that God was happy he had decided to follow Jesus once again.

Bobby stayed with me at Dr. Elma's house that night. The next morning, I asked him if he would like to move in with me and share my room. At that point, Dr. Elma was back in Finland on furlough for a few months and I was minding her house. She and I had prayed for Bobby often. I knew she would have no problem with him staying with me. Bobby agreed and left the apartment he was renting.

The two of us assumed that when Dr. Elma returned, we would have to move out and find a place of our own together. When she got back, however, she was so overjoyed to see Bobby's turnaround that she invited us both to remain with her until we left Bangladesh. We were ecstatic, and in exchange for her generosity, we helped pay the wages of the servants.

Because I was doing well financially from the currency exchange, Bobby did not even have to contribute anything for our food. This allowed him to be able to give more of his own money to God, which was a great blessing for him also.

Soon after this, Bobby signed up for a discipleship course from the International Correspondence Institute, now known as Global University (www.globaluniversity.edu), a school which offers Bible courses by correspondence. He also began to study English in anticipation of our move to Canada. In this time, he began to blossom as man of God. As he grew in Christ, a number of things started changing. Some of the friends whom he had previously alienated, and who were actually avoiding him, began to respect him again and enjoy his company. God was restoring his honour in the eyes of others. These friends started to come around looking for him, asking him to hang out with them. Bobby now had the strength to respectfully tell them that although he wanted to remain their friend, he did not want to party with them anymore. He told them he wanted to study the Word of God and to follow Christ. This was surprising to his old friends and served as a powerful testimony of Jesus Christ. With their own eyes, they saw the changes taking place in Bobby's life. They also knew they could not attribute this to anyone besides Jesus, because there had been no other cause.

Some of the other changes were practical in nature. He began to use his time more effectively. He started exercising. He looked healthier, happier, and more content. But Bobby was not the only one to benefit from his rededication to Christ. I too was blessed and full of joy to see that he was out of the slimy pit and was now standing on solid ground (Ps. 40:2).

I was surprised by how joyful I was as a result of Bobby's return to Christ. At this point, I had a little epiphany as I remembered 1 John 1:3–4: "We proclaim to you what we have seen and heard, so that you also may have fellowship with us. And our fellowship is with the Father and with his Son, Jesus Christ. We write this to make our joy complete." That passage helped me understand that the unity of fellowship between ourselves and God brings us our initial joy, and the unity of fellowship with other believers makes the joy complete. This unity had been Jesus' specific prayer for believers (John 17:20–23).

There is to be a burden on our hearts when our brothers and sisters are not walking with Christ, a burden that stirs us into action: to wake up, stand up, pray, and to intercede for them before the throne of God. When I did so, God was more than happy to answer this prayer. In this way, he not only brought glory to his own name, but he showed me that his heart was not as I had previously understood. Yes, he is God of justice and righteousness, but he did not come to earth to condemn. He came to show mercy, grace, and forgiveness. This God, who created the heavens and the earth, is filled with love for us. In fact, the Word of God says God *is* love (1 John 4:8). It does not say that He *has* love, it says he *is* love, the very source of love, the headwaters of love! As Peter writes, "The Lord is not slow in keeping his promise, as some understand slowness. He is patient with you, not wanting anyone to perish, but everyone to come to repentance" (2 Pet. 3:9).

Strangely enough, this was merely a review of the first lesson that Jesus taught me when he came to me in Pudu prison. He showed me all of the sinners of the world, but my eyes could only see their sin. This was not how he saw things. He saw the people whom he loved and who needed to hear his message of reconciliation. God loved the world so deeply that he sent his only Son to this earth, so that if we believed in him, we would not die but have eternal life (John 3:16).

This is my God. This is the One I serve. This is the God who could not bear to see his beloved perish. This same God, in the form of Jesus Christ, willingly gave his own life on the cross as redemption for mine and for yours. By his own life, he bought ours back. It is for this purpose I have been called: that I may speak to everyone possible about the heart of God the Father. This is how God loves us. It is beyond measure.

Soon after this, we were in communication with my father again. He was so happy to hear that Bobby and I were getting along and staying together again. He was also overjoyed to know that Bobby was steering clear of the partying, smoking, and drugs. Gradually, he began to accept the fact that Bobby and I were following Jesus. Seeing that Bobby's behaviour had improved so much, he began to wonder if perhaps this Jesus character was not so bad after all.

During our final period in Bangladesh, God restored my finances beyond anything I would have hoped for, he restored my brother to himself and to me, and he paved the way for full restoration with my family.

Finally, after more than two years in Bangladesh, our immigration paperwork was complete. We were interviewed at the Canadian Embassy, and after we went through the usual medical examinations, we were granted landed immigrant status.

There were a lot of tearful good-byes as we left for our new life in Canada. We learned so much from the Bangladeshi Christians. We were so sad to leave them. Bangladesh was a detour we had never expected, one that had blessed us so much. When I left Iran, I just wanted to get to North America to teach Christians about Islam, but the Lord had something different planned for me—something better: forgiveness, joy, peace, mercy, faith, hope, and, above all, love.

If you currently find yourself on a detour, let God have his way. I promise, his itinerary will be much better than the one you had planned. God bless you on your journey.

CHAPTER 16

The Challenge

My goal in writing this book was to bless you, the reader, with a new desire to draw closer to the God who created the heavens and the earth, the One who gives you life, and the One who loves you beyond anything you could ever imagine.

When I first met Pastor Asa Kain, he said, "Afshin, you must write your testimony in a book." For the past twenty years, everywhere I have gone, Christians have given me the same exhortation: "You must write your testimony!" For twenty years, I have been resistant to do so. Let me explain why.

There has never been doubt about Jesus Christ himself. All over the world, wherever you go, even if you are speaking to someone who believes that Christ never existed, the teachings that are attributed to him are held in the highest regard. Everyone can agree that his wisdom is timeless, his answers extraordinary, his compassion unfathomable, and his thinking revolutionary. No one would debate that if they put his teachings into practice, they would be elevated to a position of honour in their society no matter what era they lived in, what language they spoke, what country they were from, or what their faith background.

For those who believe in Jesus as a historical figure and believe the biblical record, there has never been any question about his power. He was a human being who has not seen an equal—a powerful teacher with an integrity and authority that has never been matched. His birth was extraordinary, his life was extraordinary, and by means of his life and death, he transformed the world. No one can debate his impact on history. Above and beyond this, by his resurrection, he transformed our relationship with God. The Bible says that Jesus Christ made the lame walk, the blind see, and the dead rise. He lifted the chin of the oppressed, fortified the weak, and broke the yoke of condemnation over the repentant sinner. But on the night he was arrested and the day that he was crucified, there was no one praising him with, "Hosanna . . . Hosanna in the highest!" as they did when He entered Jerusalem (Matt. 21:9). There is no record of anyone shouting, "We should be ashamed of ourselves! What are we doing? This is madness! Stop! This man is innocent. This man is a gift from heaven!"

The power of Jesus' ministry is not under scrutiny. Instead, the people who claim to follow Jesus are questioned. In fact, many people in the world hate Christ, not because of anything that is attributed to him, but because of Christians, or those who claim to follow Christ. What we have done in the name of Jesus Christ has damaged their perceptions of him and has hardened their hearts. Many people view Christianity as a mere religion, the church as a business, and the Bible as a way to control people.

The day that Christ came to me, he forgave me of my sin, and I felt light. I knew I was forgiven, and I was set free from chains and bondage. Prior to this, my sin had paralyzed me. I could not be what God wanted me to be. Many people had seen my former ways, and I did not want them to think that my relationship with Jesus was just a passing phase. So I refused to write my testimony until I had enough time to prove one thing—on the day that Jesus forgave me, he broke the yoke of my oppression completely. Those chains of sin fell from my wrist and ankles, and they fell off for good. I might stumble, but I would never be the same person again.

It wasn't until 2009 that I felt the blessing and the command of God in my heart to begin the process of publishing this story. This has always been a testimony for *my* life—a testimony that sustained *me.* The Bible says Christians overcame the accuser "by the blood of the Lamb and by the word of their testimony" (Rev. 12:11). The key word is "overcame." The blood of Jesus, the Lamb, is given for all, but the word of my testimony is my personal weapon and source of strength to overcome Satan, the accuser, in my life. I never expected my testimony to become a weapon for you to overcome the accuser in your life. But I pray that my story would be a source of hope and inspiration for you to embark on a journey to learn more about Jesus Christ. I want you to discover how much he loves you, and that this love has the power to release you from sin. It has the power to conquer those things that have dogged you in your life—those things that have held you captive. This love of Jesus has the power to heal wounds so deep that no medication, no technology, no surgeon, no counselling, and no psychiatrist could ever heal. This love removes the deepest and darkest of sins. God is love, and he has the power to restore you completely. When you come to a full knowledge of this, you will have your own testimony, which will serve as your weapon to overcome the accuser in your life.

I have prayed that the Lord would challenge you in a way that would be a great blessing to you. I must say that after September 11, 2001, many people approached me and said, "Now is the best time for you to write your testimony! People are reading about Islam more than ever before. It will sell like mad!" Some even dared say, "It will make you a millionaire!" (as if I cared). When I heard these words I knew that I must *not* write my book in the rabid anti-Muslim wake of 9/11. I have written this book not for financial gain but for the encouragement of those who have lost hope, to flame the fire of those who have desired more from God, and to enable those who have not looked to heaven for a long time because they believe heaven has forgotten them. I write this book to empower people to take one step closer to God, the Mighty God, the Creator of heaven and earth. If I can help just one person to trust God and move closer to his light, then I have achieved what I set out to do.

I have received the greatest riches that the heavens and the earth can offer, because I have found fulfilment in my life. Now my only desire is that you would know that there is a God, that the world was not an accident, that there is a great plan and a purpose for you, that the world's beauty is a display of the splendour of the mighty King, and that this King loves each and every one of us, the least to the greatest.

Creation is just one way he expresses his love, and the extravagance of this love is evident in the majesty of this creation. Look at photographs of the Himalayas. Who could imagine something so beautiful? Look at the photographs of the galaxies taken from space—there are at least a hundred billion stars in the Milky Way alone. Who can fathom a God so big? Look at the abundance of fish in the Great Barrier Reef and then look at the amazing creatures from the depths of the ocean trenches. Who can understand a God with such creativity? Whether you stand in the rainforest in Brazil or the deserts of Africa, every plant, every insect, every reptile, and every mammal is perfectly suited to survive and thrive in the home God has made for them. And all creatures are so beautiful in their design. The Lord did not hold back in the display of his beauty in creation. We hang photographs of mountains, sunrises, sunsets, oceans, rivers, waterfalls, flowers, animals, moonscapes, and starry skies in our homes and offices so that we can revel in their beauty and find hope and inspiration in their majesty. The Lord has shown us the extravagance of creation as a sign to us that his love is as boundless and extravagant as the beauty and diversity of this universe.

If you are a reader who does not believe in the existence of God, I want to challenge you not to read any book, attend any lecture, or talk to any professor. I want to challenge you to a simple, personal experiment—a scientific experiment of sorts. From your soul, from the deepest part of your being, humbly and respectfully ask, with all sincerity and desire, "Are you there, God? Can you really bring the freedom and life that people talk about? Would you show me in a way I can understand?" If he answers you, then you will be able to enjoy the new life that Christians speak of so passionately. If you receive no answer, then you have lost nothing—absolutely nothing. The experiment will cost you but a moment of your time. If you thought you could find meaning and satisfaction by attending expensive workshops with some self-help guru, you would spend the money gladly. In this scenario, you invest nothing but some time, and if you receive an answer, you have gained everything. This is a worthwhile investment.

If you are a Christian, but you have not sought his will in a long time, I have been praying that you would be challenged to ask him to fulfil his plan for your life. I would never have dreamed that God would do the things he has done in my life or that he would take me the places I have gone. The things he has used me for, and the ways that he has used me, have been so much better than anything I could have fathomed. It blows me away when I stop and consider it.

In the Bible he says, "'For I know the plans I have for you,' declares the LORD, 'plans to prosper you and not to harm you, plans to give you hope and a future'" (Jer. 29:11). My life is a living testimony that God can take us places we could never reach on our own. When we give him our obedience and full submission, whether we are responding to his Word or his Spirit, we receive the fullness of the life, joy, and peace he desires for us. It is only when we let our own desires die and follow him with all of our hearts that he fills us with the living water that he promises (John 4:11).

If you are from another faith background, be it Hinduism, Sikhism, Buddhism, or Islam, I don't want you to think, "Does this mean everything I have ever known is wrong?" Certainly not. Not everything that you have learned is wrong. You can find some truth in any religion. There is no question about it. Instead, I'm simply trying to point you to the source of truth: Jesus. Embrace him and he will guide you in all things.

I am often disappointed that people of other faiths have been turned off by presentations of the gospel that boil down to something like this: "Hey, you had better believe in Jesus Christ or you are going to hell." This sort of presentation of the gospel is no more hopeful than the Koran, which essentially says, "Hey, you had better believe in Allah and Mohammad or you are going to hell."

The word "gospel" literally means "good news" in Old English. The Bible says, "How beautiful on the mountains are the feet of those who bring good news, who proclaim peace, who bring good tidings"

(Isa. 52:7). It's really hard for me to see how, "Hey, you are going to hell!" could be interpreted as a beautiful message. Make no mistake, Jesus talks about hell in very blunt terms, but hell is *not* the starting point of his delivery. The starting point is the good news: "For God so loved the world that he gave his one and only Son, that whoever believes in him shall not perish but have eternal life. For God did not send his Son into the world to condemn the world, but to save the world through him. Whoever believes in him is not condemned . . ." (John 3:16–18).

Only after every man hears and understands the good news of God's love, the sacrifice of his own Son, and his freely offered forgiveness, and chooses of his own will to ignore this offer, is there any discussion of judgement: ". . . but whoever does not believe stands condemned already because he has not believed in the name of God's one and only Son" (John 3:18).

Close your eyes, go to your heart, and imagine yourself in that sweltering little concrete box that held me captive in Pudu prison. Imagine how it would have felt to have a personal audience with Jesus Christ. Quiet your mind and your spirit so that you can hear the still, small voice of this God who loves you. In the Bible, people who recognized their need, whether a leper, a tax collector, or a prostitute, were welcomed by Jesus with words of love, gentleness, humility, servanthood, forgiveness, restoration, reconciliation, and hope. This was my experience of him too, and it can be yours.

In fact, the first time Jesus spoke in a synagogue, he spoke words of hope. He read from the prophet Isaiah, "The Spirit of the Lord is on me, because he has anointed me to preach good news to the poor. He has sent me to proclaim freedom for the prisoners and recovery of sight for the blind, to release the oppressed, to proclaim the year of the Lord's favor" (Luke 4:18–19). Then he declared, "Today this scripture is fulfilled in your hearing" (Luke 4:21).

If you have rejected Christ because you have been hurt by Christians, please forgive his followers for not being more like him. In so doing, you will be the one who is acting like Christ, and how ironic would that be? Understand that everyone is a work in progress. Becoming a

Christian does not instantly make you a beautiful expositor of Jesus' good news.

Ask Jesus, "Do you have a word of encouragement for me, Jesus? Do you have a word of love for me? Do you have a word of healing? Jesus, can you help me?" I ask you this for one reason only: so that you will be blessed, as I was blessed. Jesus says, "Ask and it will be given to you; seek and you will find; knock and the door will be opened to you. For everyone who asks receives; he who seeks finds; and to him who knocks, the door will be opened" (Matt. 7:7–8). For this reason, I know that if anyone asks with all sincerity, seeks with all of his heart, and knocks with persistence, Jesus will answer. When you taste, you will see that the Lord is good.

A Concluding Thought

Wherever I go, people of all ages want to know what Jesus looks like. You will notice that I have deliberately omitted such a description from the pages of this book. There are lots of reasons for this, but the most important is that the Bible itself is also nearly silent about his appearance beyond Isaiah telling us that he was an ordinary-looking man (Isa. 53:2). It is far more important what Jesus said and did than what he looked like. Likewise, when it comes to my story, I hope you focus on Jesus' words, teaching, and compassion.

But there is one question that I am asked, wherever I go, by people of all ages and nationalities: "What colour are Jesus' eyes?" This one question I do want to answer.

When you look into Jesus' eyes, it is as if his arms reach out and grab you by the shoulders, and pull you into his being. You find yourself enveloped in an ocean of indescribable love, compassion, mercy, and grace—an ocean with no bottom and no horizon. The love and goodness stretch indefinitely in an indescribable expanse. The completion of every good thing fills this ocean: the fullness of joy, the fullness of peace, and the fullness of life. You feel like you are floating in a sea of all that is good, all that is noble, and all that is righteous. You see, there is no simple answer to the question, "What colour are his eyes?"

As David said, "Your love, O Lord, reaches to the heavens." (Ps. 36:5) That it does.

This love I describe is available to every man, woman, and child who walks upon this earth. This is the God I serve. He is my everything. "For to me, to live is Christ, and to die is gain" (Phil. 1:21). I have written this book that you would have his blessings over your life, his Word guiding you, and his Spirit as your companion for the remainder of your time on earth, until he comes back or we meet him face to face. God bless you and be with you, forever. Amen.

Oh, yes, and before I forget, do you remember that man in the shadows who looked over me when I was a boy? That was him. That was Jesus.

Afterword

Mehran and Saeed spent quite a bit more time at Pudu prison. Mehran was there for about one year and Saeed for about two. Both men were eventually accepted for immigration to European countries. Unfortunately, I have lost contact with them.

In case you were wondering, I was indeed baptized in Bangladesh by pastor Asa Kain—in the ocean actually—this was a story in itself but I will have to save it for another time.

Since moving to Canada I have lived in the greater Vancouver area. For the past five years, I have been pastor of Vancouver Christian Fellowship, a church located in North Vancouver, British Columbia. Our church Web site is **www.vancouverchristianfellowship.com** and our ministry Web site is **www.iamthirsty.ca**. If you have the opportunity, please come visit us. Mehran and Saeed, my brothers, if you are out there, please contact me. I would love to hear from you again.

Endnotes

1. And He created Jinns from fire free of smoke. (Surah 55:15)
2. He created man from sounding clay like unto pottery. (Surah 55:14)
3. See for example Surah 6:130 or 55:33.
4. See Surah 46:29 and 72:1.
5. Although at the time I believed the Jinn to be a parallel race of spirit beings above humans but below the angels and demons, in light of the Bible I now regard the Jinn as entirely demonic in nature.
6. We believe that this may have been Kerry Wiley but we are unable to confirm this fact as he now lives in seclusion.
7. Say: He is Allah, the One and Only; Allah, the Eternal, Absolute; He begets not, nor is He begotten; And there is none like unto Him. (Surah 112)
8. If you were in doubt about as to what We have revealed to you, then ask those who have been reading the Book from the Lord: so be in no wise of those in doubt. (Surah 10:94).
9. See for example Surahs 3:71, 3:78, 5:51, and 5:72–73.

10. It is not fitting for a man that Allah should speak to him except by inspiration, or from behind a veil, or by the sending of a Messenger to reveal, with Allah's permission, what Allah wills: for He is Most High, Most Wise. (Surah 42:51)
11. Throughout this book, when I have recounted passages I read in my Bible, I quoted the New International Version instead of the King James Version. I have done this because the NIV uses modern English and is therefore much easier for the reader to understand. However, my first Bible was in seventeenth-century English.